MOON MISSION

THE EPIC 400-YEAR JOURNEY TO APOLLO 11

MOON MISSION

THE EPIC 400-YEAR JOURNEY TO APOLLO 11

Sigmund Brouwer

KIDS CAN PRESS

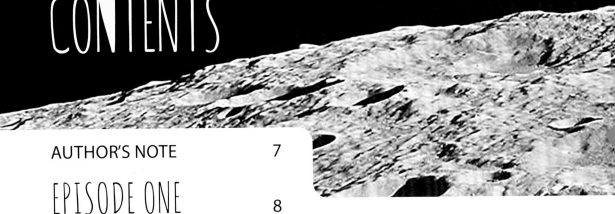

CONTENTS

Author's Note

Welcome to our epic 400-year journey to the moon and back. It may be a cliché to say that this journey was a human triumph over obstacles. Yet what makes it so incredible is that many of the obstacles were life-or-death challenges that no humans had faced before.

Again and again, as I learned more of the details behind those first steps on the moon, I marveled at how many things could have gone wrong along the way — and how many possibilities were anticipated and solved ahead of time. As you live this journey, you will no doubt be flabbergasted by the unexpected problems, and alarmed at how close the moon journey came to disaster at so many stages.

Looking back and knowing that Apollo 11 was successful makes it difficult to truly understand how back then, in July of 1969, all the watching world held its breath in fearful suspense, not knowing how the journey would end — and how we celebrated in a frenzy when we witnessed that first step on the moon.

Few observers really comprehended the dramas and dangers along the way until after the astronauts had returned. You may come to places in this book where it feels like fiction — as if yet another near disaster happens simply to add to the excitement. You probably know the ending. The real story, you will learn, is in how close it came, in so many places, to an entirely different and tragic end.

You'll see that every episode in this story has three stages — just like the *Saturn V* spacecraft had three stages. As I discovered more and more of this intriguing story, it was not difficult to imagine I was on that mission, from ignition to the moonwalk to the final splashdown and everything along the way. When you read the first stage of every episode, I hope you, too, will feel like you are one of the astronauts, and when you splash down, it seems as if you went to the moon and back yourself.

As you'll see, this journey to the moon began much earlier and took centuries of achievements along the way. In the second stage of every episode, you'll get a sense of how epic and amazing that first walk on the moon was thanks to the stories of those who pushed the boundaries of our human knowledge.

As for the third stage of each episode, I hope you have as much fun as I did learning about the science, technology, engineering and math behind the Apollo 11 mission.

So strap yourself into the space capsule and get ready for a trip to the moon and back …

Sigmund Brouwer

◄ Two months before Apollo 11, Apollo 10 was a practice trip for the first moon landing. In this North American Rockwell Corporation artist's depiction, the Apollo 10 Lunar Module descends for a closer look at the lunar landing site while the Command and Service Module remains in orbit around the moon.

HOUR   MINUTE   SECOND

EPISODE ONE

COUNTDOWN

"Two minutes, 10 seconds and counting. The target for the Apollo 11 astronauts, the moon. At liftoff we'll be at a distance of 218 096 miles away."

— *NASA transcript, Apollo 11 mission*

◄ The *Saturn V* rises from its pad at Launch Complex 39 at the Kennedy Space Center, Florida.

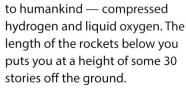

STAGE ONE: IGNITION

▼ A few hours before launch, a technician performs a last-minute task on top of the white room next to the Apollo 11 spacecraft. It's hard to see him next to the massive rocket.

It's less than nine seconds from liftoff on the morning of July 16, 1969. This is the precise moment when five F-1 rocket engines ignite beneath you.

You are locked in what is essentially a giant thermos atop a series of connected tubes filled with the most explosive fuel known to humankind — compressed hydrogen and liquid oxygen. The length of the rockets below you puts you at a height of some 30 stories off the ground.

Your training makes you an expert on gravity. You don't want to do the math but you can't help it. The rocket is so huge that if you were to jump from your perch, it would take you a full five seconds of free fall before impact. Did someone mention those rocket tubes were filled with super-cooled explosive fuels? Yes, to the point that the metal skin holding this fuel is cold enough to convert Florida humidity into ice that cakes the rocket and snow that drifts from its sides. Man-made snow. This is July, the hottest part of the year.

Ignition.

You have to be here to truly understand the volcanic explosion that sends out shock waves of sound heard hundreds of miles away. In the first second after ignition, and in each second after that, 10 000 lb. (4535 kg) of rocket fuel burns.

In a sense, the science is simple. The thrust from the engines is like air escaping a balloon — air that shoots the balloon away from the thrust.

Simple. Just combine compressed hydrogen and liquid oxygen and a flame. Let the explosion of gases create thrust for those tubes. Ensure the tubes remain vertical as this thrust tries to escape through a bottleneck at the bottom.

But the history of rockets also shows how simple it is to get it wrong. You need a big explosion, but not too big or it blows you up. You need heat, but also engines that won't burn up in that heat, and heat that won't in turn incinerate you.

Early on, rocket experiments all tended to be the same. One attempt explodes. Another attempt doesn't ignite. The third attempt rises just enough to fall and explode. The fourth goes sideways. And so on. Happily, these were mostly unmanned rockets.

But mistakes have happened with astronauts aboard, too. As the rocket below you shudders from ignition, you are highly aware of this history. You remember the tragedy of the Apollo 1 mission, when a fire during a prelaunch test killed three astronauts strapped in a similar spacecraft.

In your giant thermos, trapped with two other people, you feel what seems like the shaking of a beast trying to escape. The massive structure is held down by rings to ensure the thrust builds and the rocket doesn't topple sideways and then fizzle and shoot like fireworks gone horribly wrong.

Below, the flames hit a deflector to keep the heat from bouncing back at the rocket. Deflector. That term fails to give you a sense of its size. It weighs almost 1 300 000 lb. (590 000 kg) — more than 40 school buses crushed into a cube. The deflector is fire-proofed with a coating of volcanic ash.

▲ Thousands of people camped out on beaches and roads near the Kennedy Space Center to watch the Apollo 11 liftoff.

These flames have to be tamed or the rocket explodes.

What tames flames? Water.

Beneath the deflector is a blast pit, where a deep swimming pool has been filled with water. All of it vaporizes on contact. Nozzles refill the pool at nearly 1000 gal. (3785 L) per second. All of that water vaporizes, too. As the flames roar, fast-flowing water turns into a massive cloud of instant steam.

At the same time, from the frozen outer skin of the rocket tubes that support your giant thermos, great chunks of ice crack away and begin to cascade to the ground.

Ignition has literally created fire and ice. Smoke and vapor. And gigantic thunder, one of the loudest sounds ever created by humans, can be heard halfway across the state of Florida. The only sound louder is a nuclear blast.

You still haven't reached liftoff. That won't happen until the rings that hold down those tubes fall away and all 6 000 000 lb. (2 721 554 kg) of fuel and metal begin the fight against gravity, a foe that never relents.

A 2 mi. (3.2 km) lineup of bumper-to-bumper school buses would weigh the same as your rocket. You need 7 500 000 lb. (3 401 943 kg) of thrust to fire that kind of weight through 60 mi. (96 km) of atmosphere above you, with gravity pulling at you like a suction cup every second of that journey.

Moving the rocket and the launch tower into place required the world's largest land vehicle. But that doesn't really tell you the story. The doors of this tank-wheeled crawler-transporter were 45 stories tall. Yes. Doors 45 stories high, half the height of most skyscrapers. Inside those doors, the world's largest air conditioners had to be built and added to the crawler to prevent clouds from forming inside.

▼ The Apollo 11 *Saturn V* space vehicle is rolled out from the Vehicle Assembly Building to the Launch Complex at the Kennedy Space Center.

Crawler-transporter and rocket and launch tower formed a Goliath so painstakingly slow, movement wasn't visible during the 5 mi. (8 km) trip to the launch pad. The tracks that moved it had cleats bigger than Sherman tanks.

What's beautiful about all of this is that everything had to be anticipated by a team of engineers thousands strong.

What's frightening is that these engineers fully expect 30 000 different pieces of the rocket to fail somewhere along the way.

Ignition. You are sitting in a thermos on a barely contained volcano.

Here's what's really terrifying. On Earth, when things go wrong, you want out. But in space, when things go wrong, you desperately want to stay inside your thermos. Outer space is a vacuum of absolute cold. In an unprotected body, that will cause any external moisture — say in your open mouth — to boil. Holding your breath would cause your lungs to rupture. After you run out of oxygen, you become a floating mummy forever.

Ignition.

Liftoff has not yet begun.

In the 8.9 seconds between ignition and liftoff, there are still so many things that could go wrong for you. Wrong in a spectacular way. With the entire world watching.

You will have no chance of completing a round trip of nearly 500 200 mi. (805 000 km) through outer space if the first two feet end in explosive failure …

▲ The 363-foot-tall Apollo 11 rocket is about to be thrust into space, where it will go into orbit around the Earth and, from there, make its way to the moon. At least that's the plan.

Solve the Engineering Mystery

You are a French nobleman and chemist. It is 1778. Many scientists believe that substances that can burn contain an element called phlogiston, which is released into the air after something burns in it or someone exhales it.

Three years earlier, an English scientist told you that heating red mercuric oxide resulted in a colorless gas. It is a strange gas: candles will burn in the gas and mice locked in a chamber with the gas will survive.

You have repeated those experiments and tried new things as well. Some elements, such as sulfur, gain weight when exposed to air. Gain weight! How can this be?

Without your discovery, there is no chance that future engineers would be able to find a way to send astronauts into outer space for their amazing and epic journey.

Who are you and what did you discover?

Answer at end of the chapter.

The *Saturn V* rocket of Apollo 11's mission was essentially a giant tube filled with millions of pounds of rocket fuel. How mind-blowing that humans found a way to balance that tube upright on the flames of ignition, let alone solve every problem and obstacle on the way to the moon and back.

But this epic journey didn't begin at that moment. It wouldn't have happened at all, for example, without a man on a bicycle in a Polish border town that had just been conquered by a foreign army.

May 2, 1945. World War II was nearing an end.

Nazi Germany was in tatters.

American troops raced in from the west. Russian troops swept in from the east.

One of the biggest prizes everyone was seeking was a new invention that, six weeks earlier, Hitler had ordered destroyed to keep it from being recovered by the Allied Forces. It was a wonder weapon that some say could have won the war for Germany if it had been completed earlier — the V-2 rocket.

A scientist and engineer named Wernher von Braun was the leader of the program. At age 28, he had declared he would make it to the moon, and now, at age 33, he and his team were 25 years ahead of the formidable United States in rocket science. To defy Hitler's order, von Braun needed to engineer something just as brilliant as the V-2.

Escape.

He'd anticipated this possibility. In January of 1945, von Braun held a secret meeting with his top lieutenants and told them something that could have seen him executed if one of them decided to betray him.

Von Braun said to his lieutenants, "Germany has lost the war. But our dream of going to the moon and to other planets isn't dead. The V-2s aren't only war weapons; they can be used for space travel. To one end or another, the Russians and the Americans will want to know what we know. To which of them will it be better to leave our inheritance and our dream? We absolutely must place the baby in the right hands."

The Russians were only 50 mi. (80 km) away by then, so close that the scientists could hear the explosions of their artillery.

◀ Wernher von Braun in front of the five F-1 engines of a *Saturn V* launch vehicle. The enormous engines powered the *Saturn V* S-IC first stage, or booster stage, of the rocket. Von Braun directed the development of the *Saturn V* and had a huge influence on America's space program.

Shortly after Hitler gave orders to destroy everything, the scientists decided to flee in the opposite direction, to the Americans. Their journey, the "Vengeance Express," took a secret convoy of trains, trucks and even barges to cross Hitler's dying empire. They hid 28 000 lb. (12 700 kg) of critical documents in an abandoned mine and took hundreds of V-2s, the launchers and test-firing rigs, and 720 000 lb. (326 600 kg) of rocket components.

They also took along Wernher's brother Magnus von Braun, who on May 2 cycled up to an American soldier in a sentry position at the newly U.S.-controlled border of Austria. Magnus told the sentry that on the other side of the mountain behind him was the inventor of the famed V-2 wonder weapon, a team of 400 rocket scientists and the inventory of the project.

Magnus was told to offer their surrender to the Americans, along with the advanced technology that Hitler wanted destroyed.

They were in great danger, Magnus explained. Nazi SS troops had orders to kill every one of them to ensure those rockets and documents and scientists would not reach the Americans. Wernher had sent his brother Magnus over the mountain because he spoke the best English. Magnus had been instructed to offer their surrender to the Americans, along with the advanced technology that Hitler wanted destroyed, and that the Russians wanted so they could vault ahead of the Americans in an arms race.

This was truly a historic moment, with the future of two superpowers in balance.

The sentry ignored Magnus von Braun, turned to other American soldiers nearby and said: "Hey, I've got a nut here! What should I do with him?"

Indeed, the first few seconds of liftoff on July 16, 1969, might never have happened because of the disbelief of a lowly private 24 years earlier in the Austrian mountains. But finally, a day later, someone in higher command understood the huge significance of the Vengeance Express. Wernher von Braun's name was at the top of a secret code–named list of German scientists and engineers wanted for interrogation by U.S. military experts.

Once the Americans knew the offer was real, they still had to smuggle the Vengeance Express out of Germany knowing that the Russians were in ruthless pursuit.

Thus marked the beginning of the Cold War and an epic decades-long race between two superpowers, between East and West, dictators and presidents, communism and democracy.

Who would get to the moon first?

You know the ending, of course. The American astronauts. Neil Armstrong. Behind him, Buzz Aldrin.

But as you can see, there is much, much more to the Apollo 11 trip than knowing the ending.

So now that you are strapped in and seconds away from liftoff, come along for the entire journey, beginning with the scientist who succeeded only because his partner died of a burst bladder. You'll meet him after you survive liftoff in the *Saturn V*.

STAGE THREE: MOON TEAM

BUZZ ALDRIN

"Whenever I gaze up at the moon, I feel like I'm on a time machine. I am back to that precious pinpoint of time, standing on the foreboding — yet beautiful — Sea of Tranquility. I could see our shining blue planet Earth poised in the darkness of space."

He was born Edwin Eugene Aldrin Jr. in 1930, but the world knows him as Buzz. He was a pilot in the U.S. Air Force, and it was decided that having a military man on the moon first would send the wrong message, so Buzz followed Neil Armstrong as the second human to walk on the moon.

Aldrin was the Lunar Module (the *Eagle*) pilot for the Apollo 11 mission. During an earlier mission (Gemini 12), he spent five hours in outer space in his space suit, proving that extravehicular activity would be possible and practical for future missions.

NEIL ARMSTRONG

"I think we're going to the moon because it's in the nature of the human being to face challenges. It's by the nature of his deep inner soul ... we're required to do these things just as salmon swim upstream."

He was an aerospace engineer, a naval aviator, a test pilot and a university professor. Neil Alden Armstrong was also the first man to walk on the moon, with a two-and-a-half-hour stroll in his space suit.

Armstrong was the mission commander for the Apollo 11 mission. He believed he had only a 50-50 chance of surviving the trip from the spaceship down to the moon. The *Eagle* had just enough fuel to land and return. The slightest of errors meant he and Aldrin would either crash back on the moon or be stranded in low orbit, floating circles around the moon for all of eternity.

Michael Collins

"We are off! And do we know it, not just because the world is yelling 'Liftoff' in our ears, but because the seats of our pants tell us so! Trust your instruments, not your body, the modern pilot is always told, but this beast is best felt. Shake, rattle and roll!"

Sometimes called the forgotten astronaut, Michael Collins was the Command Module pilot for Apollo 11. He stayed in the Command Module (the *Columbia*), traveling in orbit around the moon, while Armstrong and Aldrin flew in the Lunar Module (the *Eagle*) to make the first manned landing on its surface. (The illustration on page 18 shows the parts of the *Saturn V*, including the Command and Service Module and the Lunar Module.)

Collins's secret terror was that Armstrong and Aldrin would face disaster on the moon's surface and he would have to fly back to Earth alone.

After all, if the *Eagle*'s engine failed to ignite, Armstrong and Aldrin would be stranded on the moon to die when their oxygen ran out. Or if it crashed, he would have no way to rescue them.

Engineering Mystery Solved

Congratulations, Antoine-Laurent de Lavoisier!

You believe that air is divided into components. One part — oxygen — will combine with other elements, thus adding weight. This same gas will also support combustion and allow animals to breathe. Another part of air will not do either of these things. You prove that phlogiston does not exist and that the atmosphere has distinct elements. Through this, you show the world the nature of oxygen and its activity in chemistry. It is a revolution in the understanding of chemistry.

Your breakthrough leads also to understanding how oxygen and hydrogen work together, either as water (H_2O) or, eventually, as the rocket fuel engineers will use for thrust.

Your noble background works against you, though, because France is going through revolutionary times and you are falsely accused of tax fraud. You are eventually proven innocent, but only after you are put to death by guillotine.

Saturn V Launch Vehicle

No other operational space rocket has been taller, heavier or more powerful than the *Saturn V*. (The "V" is a Roman numeral and is pronounced "five.") It's the only vehicle to have ever moved humans beyond low Earth orbit. Weighing in at over 6.5 million pounds (nearly 3 million kilograms), it still flew more than 30 times faster than the speed of sound.

Second Stage

After stage one drops away, the second stage's J-2 engines ignite. Thirty seconds after that, the launch escape tower is discarded to save weight. Stage two (S-II) engines thrust the *Saturn V* to an altitude of 114.5 mi. (184 km).

First Stage

With over a half million gallons (about 2 million liters) of rocket fuel, stage one (S-IC) pushes the *Saturn V* to a height of 38 mi. (61 km) before the engines shut down. Then, explosive bolts fire so that this stage breaks away and falls to the ocean.

Interstage Adaptor

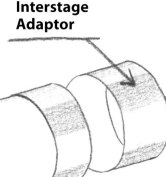

Five J-2 Engines

Five F-1 Engines

If you set the *Saturn V* on its side on your school playground, you could line up ten school buses from tip to tip. Of that entire length, the *Columbia* Command Module and *Eagle* Lunar Module would fit in just one of those buses. Most of the length of the *Saturn V* was needed for rocket fuel. Each of the three stages was wide enough to park four school buses beside each other with room left over.

Third Stage

Stage three (S-IVB) first burns for only two minutes — long enough to put the spacecraft into orbit around Earth. When it shuts down, the astronauts check all the equipment. Then the rocket reignites to thrust the Command and Service Module and the Lunar Module together out of Earth's orbit and toward the moon.

Escape Rocket

If the launch goes wrong, the escape rocket will ignite with a large but brief thrust to pull the CSM and the astronauts inside it away from the *Saturn V* to safety.

Lunar Module Adaptor

One J-2 Engine

Command and Service Module

The *Columbia* is the Apollo 11 Command Module and the only part of the *Saturn V* to return to Earth. The Command Module is home for the three astronauts on the way to the moon and back. A Service Module, which contains fuel, electrical power, oxygen and water, is attached to the bottom of the *Columbia*. Together, these are called the Command and Service Module (CSM). On the trip home, the Service Module is cast off and allowed to burn up in the atmosphere.

Lunar Module

The Lunar Module (LM), the *Eagle*, was designed to ferry two astronauts from the Command and Service Module (CSM) to the moon and back. After stage three blasts both modules into escape velocity, the astronauts connect the *Columbia* to the *Eagle* for the journey to the moon.

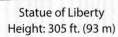

Statue of Liberty
Height: 305 ft. (93 m)

Saturn V Spacecraft
Height: 363 ft. (111 m)

Human
(to Scale)

00:00:00

HOUR   MINUTE   SECOND

EPISODE TWO

LIFTOFF

"Ten, 9, ignition sequence start, 6, 5, 4, 3, 2, 1, zero. All engines running. Liftoff! We have a liftoff! Thirty-two minutes past the hour. Liftoff on Apollo 11!!"

— *NASA transcript, Apollo 11 mission*

◀ A camera mounted on the mobile launch tower captured this view of the Apollo 11 rocket lifting off at 9:32 a.m. EDT on July 16, 1969.

STAGE ONE: HUMAN BULLET

▼ The Apollo 11 crew, Armstrong, Collins and Aldrin, leave the Kennedy Space Center Manned Spacecraft Operations Building. The prelaunch countdown is on.

Disaster. Total disaster.

During the final seconds before liftoff, it feels like you are a helpless rat in the mouth of a giant terrier shaking you from side to side. Against the violent shuddering of the massive rocket trying to escape gravity, the millions of parts must hold together or all the fuel will trigger one of the biggest non-nuclear bombs in human history.

First, there is one slow, minuscule movement of liftoff … It's a fractional gap between the massive rocket and the launch pad.

Then another tiny sliver … Then …

One part fails. Just one part. It's a fuel line with liquid oxygen, and it snaps apart.

The oxygen is super cooled and pours downward like streams of water reaching for first contact with the rocket's overheated engines.

There is a spark.

Within a blink, the world's mightiest rocket tears itself apart in a mushrooming burst of red flames, spewing wreckage in all directions. Imagine driving away for half an hour at highway speed — that's as

NO SMOKING

far as some of the wreckage will finally land. Some of the flames claw upward, higher than the top of any thundercloud. In the stunning silence of the aftermath, as the rocket burns itself out for nearly an hour, droplets of fuel drift down like oily rain.

This is not something in your imagination. This is not a worst-case scenario.

It's real. It happened in the Soviet Union 12 days before your own launch.

On July 3, a U.S. spy satellite passed overhead and took photos showing that the Soviets had moved an N-1 rocket ship into place. It was part of a space program so secretive that the moon race was too close to call.

The next pass of the satellite, however, delivered photos with a strange blur — and a huge scar on the ground where the rocket had stood.

It was a total disaster — the giant rocket destroyed — simply because of a snapped oxygen line.

Inside your capsule, you know this happened to the Soviets. And you know you have to trust the American technology. And the American engineers.

The week before your own ignition and launch, something on your rocket was leaking. The engineers had traced it to your

main liquid oxygen tank. They were looking at four days of repair, which would have canceled your launch. Then a technician tightened a nut and the problem was fixed. So they went back to the 1700-page launch control plan and kept counting down to this moment of liftoff.

You are hooked up to oxygen lines. You are in lap belts and shoulder harnesses. It took a 417-point checklist just to get you seated inside the cabin.

Now there is no stopping the countdown. You will either launch — or destruct.

▲ The Apollo 11 astronauts practice an emergency egress, so they are prepared to escape quickly and safely if necessary.

▲ The *Saturn V* at liftoff and a few seconds later

As the thunder of ignition fills your ears, you can picture the 30-story rocket fighting the hold-down arms locking it in place. Massive amounts of thrust are needed just to stabilize the rocket. Until that moment, the danger is that the rocket will topple. The concept is the same as holding the brakes and spinning the rear tires of a race car. When the brakes are released, the car will explode forward.

You can't feel it, but at T minus zero, the hold-down arms begin to fall away.

You can't feel it, but slowly the rocket moves upward — so slowly, and for just a couple of seconds.

In 60 seconds, the rocket will have disappeared from the view of Earth, leaving behind a trail of exhaust from a blinding white flare. In 90 seconds, the continued acceleration away from the launch pad will be so violent that the skin on your neck will flap and your eyes will be squeezed into egg shapes by the force of gravity.

But that is 60 seconds away. And 90 seconds away. After a successful launch. There are no guarantees this will be successful.

You are too aware of what happened to the Soviet spaceship almost two weeks earlier. You know that you still have to clear the rocket tower in the moments following liftoff.

You also know that in the next few seconds, your thermos-shaped cabin might well be flung from the top of the rocket toward the ocean. The launch escape tower has been prepared: at the first inkling of disaster, it will fire you toward the ocean. But only if there is time. Otherwise, your body will become carbon dust, floating down with the drops of unburned rocket fuel.

The rattling and shaking become so intense that you close your eyes. You are helpless to do anything else.

And then, in a great whoosh, you feel the acceleration, like the reverse of being dropped down a roller coaster, except with triple the force.

You'd smile, but it's impossible. G-forces stretch your lips across your face.

One minute and 21 seconds later, your rocket is moving at 1800 mi. (2900 km) per hour — that's 2640 ft. (805 m) per second. Less than a minute later, you've tripled that speed. As every second passes, you leave the launch pad another 1½ mi. (2.4 km) behind. You are a human traveling faster than a bullet.

Ahead of you is the edge of the bubble of Earth's atmosphere.

Outer space.

Solve the Science Mystery

You broke the Missouri state record in high jump as a student in 1906, and as a boxer, you once knocked out a German heavyweight champion. You're also a former high-school basketball coach and law student who served in World War I. Leaving all that behind, you spend the early 1920s looking at the night sky through a massive telescope atop Mount Wilson in southern California.

Who would expect, with a background like that, you would change how humans understand the scope of the universe? Until then, we believed the universe consisted only of our galaxy, the Milky Way. On December 30, 1924, you announce you have found conclusive evidence that what we once thought were stars are actually other galaxies. Millions upon millions of galaxies. Your discovery earns you the title of greatest astronomer since Galileo.

Something bothers you, however. You know that when a wave of light shortens, it becomes more blue. When it lengthens, it becomes more red. Through that massive telescope, you observe that light from every star and every galaxy is shifting to red. There is only one conclusion. The stars and galaxies are moving away from us. In every direction. The universe is expanding. And every galaxy in every direction is expanding at a greater speed each year.

Who are you, and what could possibly be going on?

Answer at end of the chapter.

STAGE TWO: A MOOSE, A GOLDEN NOSE AND A BURST BLADDER

It's not much of a stretch — pun intended — to say that a burst bladder led to confirmation of one of the greatest shifts in human understanding of the solar system. Without this shift, a moon landing would have been impossible.

The epic journey to the moon, then, began centuries earlier with a Polish scientist named Mikołaj Kopernik. He is known to us as Nicolaus Copernicus, and he needed help from beyond his own grave from a man with a nose made of brass, a man who died because of, yes, that burst bladder.

▲ Nicolaus Copernicus was an astronomer and mathematician. He believed that the sun and not the Earth was the center of our universe.

Copernicus lived at a time when everyone was taught that Earth was at the center of the universe and that the sun and planets circled around it. This was the way science had viewed the heavens for centuries. It's safe to argue that no moon journey would ever be successful if we first didn't understand the way objects move around in space. Someone had to prove beyond a doubt the revolutionary notion that the planets revolve around the sun.

Copernicus wrote a book outlining this theory, but it wasn't published until shortly before he died. He was too afraid of the religious establishment, which disagreed with him and had so much power that some 50 years after his book was published, only a handful of astronomers were brave enough to publicly agree with Copernicus that the planets orbit the sun. Better proof was needed to make this a foundation of science, because part of the difficulty of the theory was that the presumed orbits of the planets were considered unpredictable.

One of that handful of astronomers who agreed with Copernicus was Tycho Brahe, who was born into a rich family in 1546, only three years after Copernicus died. Having money mattered because Brahe was a true geek, and his inheritance allowed him the luxury of spending time on an island between

Denmark and Sweden, making detailed notes about the positions of planets and stars. This was before the invention of the telescope, and he claimed himself to be the greatest observer of the skies who ever lived.

Brahe, however, wasn't so good at the mathematics required to convert the movement of the planets into predictable orbits.

Happily, Brahe met a German scientist named Johannes Kepler, who was great at mathematics but not so great at collecting data. The two of them would have made perfect partners.

Unhappily, though, Brahe loved to party and Kepler, well, not so much. Kepler was an introvert and Brahe, who at one time kept a pet moose in his house, was not. The one story that gives insight into Brahe's personality is how he lost the tip of his nose. It was because of a drunken argument with a fellow university student over who was better at math. The argument led to a duel, where Brahe proved he was also second place at sword-fighting, and for the rest of his life, he wore a brass nose.

Given this conflict in personalities, it's no surprise that Kepler and Brahe didn't like each other. Brahe would pass along only a few of his notes at a time to Kepler.

Unhappily, Kepler could not make progress in his work without all of Brahe's data. Happily — and unhappily — Kepler acquired all of Brahe's notes because of the one time and place that Brahe should not have had too much beer.

It was an evening party where the guest of honor was a Danish nobleman. Despite an urgent need to relieve his bladder, Brahe could not respectfully excuse himself from the baron's presence. Brahe held off on relieving himself for so long that his bladder burst inside his body. He died soon after from internal infection. His last words were to Kepler: "Let me not seem to have lived in vain."

Fifty years after his book was published, only a handful of astronomers were brave enough to agree that the planets orbit the sun.

Kepler did ensure Brahe's life meant something. Armed with all the data he needed from Brahe, Kepler proposed his famous laws of planetary motion, which proved Copernicus correct beyond a doubt and should have immediately upended the traditional view of science on Earth's place in the universe.

Except.

This was a time of superstition. Kepler made money by publishing calendars that predicted planetary positions with such uncanny accuracy that his final calendar was burned in public. Indeed, Kepler had to postpone his work to focus on successfully defending his own mother against witchcraft charges.

By this point, the moon really needed someone persuasive to tell the story of its journey — someone who would later be known as the father of modern science.

Someone who would be Galileo Galilei. More about him after you've managed to escape Earth's gravity.

STAGE THREE: GRAVITY — THE FORCE IS WITH YOU (AND AGAINST YOU)

Rest your hands on a table. Leave all your fingers flat as you raise the pinkie of your right hand.

There.

You've just defeated one of the four major forces of the universe. Don't cheer. It's only a temporary victory. While gravity is millions upon millions upon millions of times weaker than the other three forces of the universe, eventually it will defeat your pinkie. Sooner or later, your pinkie will have to return to its lowest point, drawn by an invisible attraction to the weight — or mass — of the entire planet.

Modern physics tells us that there are four distinct forces in the universe. Two of them don't seem obvious in our daily lives. These are the strong nuclear force and the weak nuclear force. Each of them is like a glue. The strong force holds the nucleus (center) of an atom together, and the weak force holds electrons to the nucleus and allows for atoms to form into more complex molecules. For example, water consists of two hydrogen atoms "glued" to one oxygen atom (H_2O). The weak nuclear force makes it relatively easy to break the hydrogen away from the oxygen. All you need to do is pass an electrical current through the water, and it will produce the two gases of hydrogen and oxygen.

It's not at all easy to break apart the strong nuclear force of an atom. When it's done, the energy released is astounding. That energy is what powered the nuclear bombs dropped on Japan in World War II.

The third force is more obvious in our

▲ Lunar Module pilot Edwin "Buzz" Aldrin goes through zero-gravity training aboard a U.S. Air Force KC-135 jet aircraft.

daily lives: electromagnetism — electricity and magnetism. Electricity can create magnetism, and magnetism can create electricity, and that's why physics considers it a single force.

It's the fourth force, gravity, that operates outside of your body. It's pulling your pinkie in a direction that we think of as downward, but the truth is your pinkie is also pulling the Earth upward toward it.

Yes, to safely land on the moon, we need an understanding of planetary orbits. But we also need a clear understanding of gravity, the force that your pinkie can defeat (but not for long).

What we know about gravity is this: It's the mutual attraction of any two objects. The bigger of the two objects will have more pull than the smaller object. The greater the distance between the two, the smaller the gravitational force.

This attraction means the planets stay in orbit, attracted to the mass of the sun. It means you stay on the ground, attracted to the mass of the much larger Earth (which is, of course, much larger than you are).

Simple, right? So simple that Isaac Newton was able to come up with a mathematical formula that lets us accurately predict the motions of all kinds of moving objects, from a baseball to the moon.

Except, if you don't want your mind blown, stay away from any more deep thoughts about gravity. Gravity pulls on matter, all matter. It forms galaxies and stars. (The sun is so big that gravity mashes hydrogen atoms into helium atoms, causing nuclear fission that releases the heat and energy keeping us alive.) Yet gravity is — get ready to count the zeroes — this much weaker than the weak nuclear force: 1 000 000 000 000 000 000 000 000 000 000 000 000 times.

Gravity works at a distance but seems to have instant attraction, even with objects millions of miles apart.

It also curves space, and causes time to slow down or speed up. Yes, to repeat, gravity curves space and time.

The other three forces have push and pull. Gravity only pulls. We have no idea why.

Gravity acts between any two forces, no matter how small or far apart. Did you drop a dime in a crack in a sidewalk on vacation in New York five years ago? Right at this moment, that dime is giving the slightest of pulls on each blade of grass in your school playground. As you walk, your body is making the tiniest of tugs on the gases of the stars half a galaxy away.

Oh, and one other thing.

Nobody has any provable theory of why gravity does what it does.

It's just … the Force.

▶ Much of the credit for Hubble's astounding new perspective on the universe goes to Henrietta Swan Leavitt. In the 1890s, she examined photographic plates of stars and came up with a system to measure the brightness and distance of the stars. Hubble, who used her work after her death, thought she deserved a Nobel prize. Sadly, her contributions to astronomy were not recognized during her lifetime.

SCIENCE MYSTERY SOLVED

Congratulations, Edwin Hubble!

The famous Hubble Space Telescope, which allows today's astronomers to see great distances into the universe, farther than you dreamed possible, is named after you.

In 1929, in your first published paper, you started a major revolution into understanding the universe. Yes, you told us that the universe is expanding all the time.

You showed us that the farther away a galaxy is, the faster the galaxy is moving, and that all galaxies are moving away from all other galaxies. And you showed us that all these galaxies continue to gain in speed as the universe expands.

How mind-expanding!

These revelations lead to even bigger questions — the why and the how questions — inspired by the kind of human curiosity that sent our astronauts to the moon on that amazing and epic journey.

As for the expanding universe? That did lead to another science mystery that needed solving. For this one, as you'll find out, the solution begins with the removal of pigeon droppings …

+ 00:02:40

HOUR   MINUTE   SECOND

EPISODE THREE

ESCAPING EARTH

"Hey, Houston, Apollo 11.
This Saturn gave us a magnificent ride."

— *NASA transcript, Apollo 11 mission*

◄ The Apollo 11 Command and Service Module

STAGE ONE: MAX-Q SURVIVAL

Barely 60 seconds after liftoff, you wish you could take a deep breath of relief. Your rocket didn't topple or explode. You didn't vaporize into a thin cloud of carbon dust, drifting across the spectators below — the spectators who are now instead seeing the last of your flames as you are hurled toward the moon.

But you don't try taking the deep breath you deserve. For one thing, your lungs can't expand against the smothering sensation of a giant palm pressing harder and harder against your ribs, its giant fingers reaching up from there to squish your eyeballs.

This feeling is an illusion. Nothing is pressing down against you. Instead, the sensation comes from below: the thrust of five rocket engines pushing upward against your body. In the time it would take for you to exhale just one deep breath — if you could — those engines would have burned enough fuel for a jet to fly across the Atlantic.

This thrust means your capsule sits on hundreds of thousands of pounds of a 30-story structure now moving faster than a .44 Magnum bullet fired from a revolver.

There is another reason you can't take a deep breath of relief. In the next few seconds, you face a further moment of truth.

You are still accelerating, pushing so hard against the atmosphere that your tiny capsule on top of the rocket compresses the air in front of it. You are about to hit maximum dynamic pressure (Max-Q). Max-Q is the combination of speed and friction against the density of atmosphere that puts maximum strain on the frame and the millions of parts that make up the structure of your rocket.

▼ The Apollo 11 mission was important to the American people. The cloudy band around the center of the spacecraft is caused by the difference in temperature between the rocket propellants and the atmosphere.

The vibration of the rocket straining against these forces is what makes the skin on your neck flap. The pressure makes it impossible to even move the muscles of your face. At this point, if you die, you won't even know it happened.

Then your eyeballs seem to drop deep into your sockets. That's a welcome sensation because it tells you, two minutes into your journey, that you are still alive, some 37 mi. (60 km) above Earth, where the atmosphere has thinned enough to take you past Max-Q to a point of relative safety.

Except. That blast from the booster was only stage one. There are still two more stages of rocket ignition.

Even though you expect it, there is nothing that can prepare you for what happens next, as the five engines silence themselves, the acceleration instantly stops and the rocket ship coasts for just one second. Brief as this is, as the pressure against you pauses for about a heartbeat, the shape of your eyeballs changes again: they suddenly bulge outward from your head.

▲ Workers in the Vehicle Assembly Building at NASA's Kennedy Space Center prepare the first stage of the *Saturn V*, the S-IC booster.

GET TIME

NASA measures time after liftoff as Ground Elapsed Time (GET). That's why, at 60 seconds, or one minute, after liftoff, you are at GET 00:01:00. The big clock the crowds at Cape Canaveral see shows the time as "minus" before liftoff and "plus" after liftoff. So the big clock now reads +00:01:00. Not that you can see it as you are whizzing by!

▼ The S-II second stage of the *Saturn V* is stacked on the first stage (S-IC).

▲ The S-IVB third stage of the rocket is moved into position for mating with the second stage (S-II).

What you see in front of you is a sudden fireball.

Your rocket has not exploded. This mushroom of flame comes from the last of your burned fuel, moving so quickly that it rushes around and past your capsule just before the boost from the next stage of rocket engines accelerates you again.

All of this happens in less than a second. As the bottom 13 stories of rocket structure — stage one — fall away, the rocket engines of stage two are exposed, and now, in a new fury, they explode. This blast drives you upward into and through the blossom of fire from the death of stage one.

You surge forward again, the giant's hand on your chest and the inward pressure squeezing your eyeballs again. And your rocket ship is still gaining speed.

Just past the nine-minute mark, you have reached an altitude of 610 000 ft. (185 928 m). You are traveling at almost 10 times the speed of a bullet fired from the most powerful rifle on the planet — with one more set of rocket engines waiting in reserve to hurl you away from Earth and into the solar system.

Soon, you will be able to breathe normally. The technology to get you this far has been incredible, yet compared to what you'll need to get through the next few hours, it will seem like moving from a wooden rowboat to a sleek battleship.

▶ The Apollo 11 Command and Service Module will be moved to the Vehicle Assembly Building and mated to the Lunar Module adapter.

Solve the Science Mystery

You are two radio astronomers in New Jersey in 1964. You are working in Bell Labs with a big antenna to detect faint radio waves that are bouncing off satellites. This means you have to filter out any and all interference, including radar and radio broadcasting. You even go to the extreme of removing heat waves from the receiver by cooling it with liquid helium.

But you have a problem. No matter where you point your antenna, you find a low, steady, mysterious noise spread evenly across the sky. It happens day or night.

You are so desperate to fix the problem that when you find pigeons nesting in the big antenna, you remove them and clean up the bird droppings, hoping they were the mysterious source of the steady noise.

Still, the noise continues and you can't find a source for it. You begin to believe this sound is coming from outside our own galaxy.

Who are you, and what could possibly be happening?

Answer at end of the chapter.

Galileo Galilei. He is surly, sarcastic and impatient. Oh, and nearly always right. That's not a good combination if you want friends, especially friends in high places.

A generation or so after Kepler, Galileo faced the same entrenched religious establishment that would not permit followers to believe the sun might be the center of the solar system.

But he had a bigger enemy than the Church: a man who had lived and died 2000 years earlier, the man then considered the greatest thinker throughout history. A Greek named Aristotle.

Aristotle, and his followers in centuries after, believed that all scientific knowledge could come from careful, reasoned thought. Galileo was essentially the first scientist to break with this philosophy. (Imagine how ingrained it was after centuries upon centuries of blind acceptance.)

For example, Aristotle taught that heavier objects would fall faster than lighter objects because it made sense.

Galileo thought that scientific knowledge should come from experimentation, not just reasoning. By using balls of different weights and measuring the rate at which they rolled down inclined planes, Galileo, it is told, proved Aristotle's teaching false.

When Galileo was mocked for believing that air had weight, he took a leather bladder filled with air and put in on a scale, balancing the weight. Then he jabbed a dagger in the leather bladder. As the air escaped, the astounded spectators watched the scale tip, plainly showing the bladder had lost weight.

By sketching sunspots (dark spots that sometimes appear on the surface of the sun) after watching them through his telescope over a period of two years, Galileo concluded that the sun rotates once every 27 days. Until then, many scientists had believed that sunspots were objects passing in front of the sun. Part of their reasoning was based on theology: God had created the sun perfectly; therefore, it could not have blemishes.

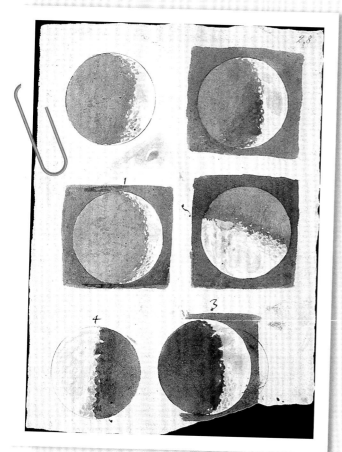

▲ Galileo's sketches of the moon's phases

Galileo's approach made him unpopular with those in power, but he was more interested in scientific truth. If proving the truth meant showing that others were wrong, so be it.

As for that telescope, Galileo didn't invent it. He merely improved it; in fact, he improved it so much that he was astounded when he saw the lunar craters — he was the first person to do so. He could foresee that, thanks to the telescope, Copernicus and Kepler would soon be proven right and the religious establishment's view of the solar system would be proven wrong.

And so, against the wishes of the Church, he published his scientific views, boldly declaring that Earth moves around the sun.

Galileo Galilei

But Galileo made a big mistake.

He misjudged the politics of his time. For daring to disagree with the religious establishment, he was arrested and faced trial, where he was condemned to house arrest for the remainder of his life.

The story goes that after the trial, when Galileo was forced to kneel and declare his views were wrong, he whispered these Latin words: *Eppur si muove* — "And yet it does move."

Although it seemed Galileo had lost, his work had lasting effects. Thanks to Copernicus and Brahe and Kepler and Galileo, science built on a foundation of superstition and religious mistrust was damaged beyond repair.

The new foundation would be built upon experiments and theories that could be tested and proven. It was a foundation that would lead humankind to those

> Galileo didn't invent the telescope; he merely improved it so much that he was astounded when he saw the lunar craters.

famous first steps on the moon. First, though, someone had to solve another of science's major mysteries: the laws of motion. The world would have to wait awhile for the twisted genius of a man who wanted to communicate with the dead.

That person would be Isaac Newton. But if you want to meet him, you need to first manage an orbit or two around Earth without drowning.

Stage Three: Columbia's Primitive On-board Computer

Stand in your classroom and hold a basketball above your head. That's planet Earth. Have someone else stand on the other side of the room and hold a marble. That's the moon. Have a third person stand in the middle and hold a piece of paper sideways so that the other two only see the thin edge. The width of the paper in comparison to those two objects, according to one astronaut, should give you an idea of the narrowness of the corridor the astronauts had to follow to the moon and back in the Command and Service Module (CSM) mother ship *Columbia* and the attached Lunar Module *Eagle*. And keep in mind that both the Earth and moon are circling the sun at a tremendous speed, so the journey through this corridor must be planned out to match both orbits.

The astronauts — who for the most part began their careers as pilots — would have liked to have flown the CSM manually. However, they needed to rely on the *Columbia*'s Apollo Guidance Computer (AGC) to navigate this precise corridor over a distance of more than 200 000 mi. (322 000 km).

At Mission Control in Houston, there were more than 3500 computer technicians using the most up-to-date computers at the time to help guide the *Columbia*. But on the *Columbia* itself, the AGC available to the astronauts had less computer power than a pocket calculator and was even more basic than many modern toasters. To put in commands, there was no arrow key or mouse or touch control. Instead, on a simple keypad, they had to enter simple nouns and verbs as code words.

Today, it's hard to believe the mission depended on a computer that primitive, especially when so many people today can't even find a restaurant across town without the help of a handheld device with a map and GPS system!

▲ This interior view of the Apollo 11 Lunar Module shows displays, controls and, mounted at the window, a 16 mm data acquisition camera.

▲ The Mission Operations Control Room at Mission Control Center, Houston, while Apollo 11 astronauts Armstrong and Aldrin are walking on the moon.

Science Mystery Solved

**Congratulations,
Arno Penzias and Robert Wilson!**

You have just proved, almost beyond a doubt, how the universe began.

Before now, scientists fought over two theories: one, that ours was a steady-state universe, one that had existed forever; and the other, that our universe had a definite beginning.

Some argued that Hubble's discovery of the expanding universe just meant the universe went back and forth between shrinking and enlarging. Others believed that if the universe was expanding outward and gaining speed as it expanded, at one point, it would have begun with an explosion — or a "big bang."

Penzias and Wilson heard about a yet-to-be-published paper that asked if there would be any radiation left over from the big bang. The two scientists realized that what they had discovered about the universe matched exactly what this paper predicted. There was a low level of microwave radiation all across the universe that made it almost certain the universe had begun with an explosion billions of years ago.

For that, Penzias and Wilson received a Nobel Prize. As for our astronauts, their epic journey is just one more puzzle piece in the picture of our universe we humans are trying to put together.

+00:11:11

HOUR   MINUTE   SECOND

EPISODE FOUR

EARTH ORBIT

"Hey, Charlie, I can see the snow on the mountains out in California, and it looks like LA doesn't have much of a smog problem today."

— *NASA transcript, Apollo 11 mission*

◄ In 10 days of Earth orbit in March 1969, the Apollo 9 mission tested systems essential for a moon landing.

STAGE ONE: DANGER IN ZERO GRAVITY

▼ This amazing photograph was taken from the Apollo 11 spacecraft on its journey to the moon, almost 112 800 mi. (181 500 km) from Earth. It shows most of Africa and parts of Europe and Asia.

Not even 12 minutes have passed since ignition. Your head points to Earth and your feet at the stars. Your greatest fear is that you will drown. Yes, drown. But you have to focus on your mission, so you try to push aside your fear.

The three of you are in bulky space suits in the CSM, still strapped into position, flying upside down. Except now there is no up or down, something that will become real to you when you finally reach the relative safety of orbit and are free to unbuckle the straps and move around inside your capsule.

A radio call from Houston reaches you. Mission Control has been checking all the data streaming back to their computers.

You hear these words: "Apollo 11 is go for orbit."

The price of escaping Earth was the violence of the engines hurling you upward. You need to inspect the CSM to make sure that any damage is minimal.

The next part of your journey will be to circle Earth one and a half times, at a height of more than 100 mi. (160 km) above the oceans, mountains, deserts, forests and cities. During this time, you and Mission Control will make sure that your equipment is ready for the great journey ahead.

Your mission and, indeed, your survival now depend on the same ancient technology that sailors once used to navigate the oceans.

This is your sextant — its design is based on the centuries-old navigational device used by sailors at sea — and you are upside down because you need to scan the stars in the same way sailors of old did.

It seems fitting, in a way. You have your own inhospitable ocean to cross, as did they — theirs was measured in thousands of miles and yours in hundreds of thousands.

The sextant measures the angle between distant objects (such as the moon and the horizon). Imagine your space module is like a bullet, and with the next firing of the rocket engines, you will shoot down the rifle barrel. Your sextant, officially called the Alignment Optical Telescope, is a little more sophisticated. You need to aim your sight on the distant stars to take the correct path to the moon.

A bullet aimed from a stationary rifle at a stationary target a half-mile away will arrive in seconds and yet miss by dozens of yards if the angle is slightly off. Your task is much, much more difficult. You are aiming from a moving object and need to hit a target zipping at over 2200 mi. (3540 km) per hour, and your bullet won't reach it for 66 hours.

The moon is big. But space is infinitely bigger. (And you are the bullet.)

If you miscalculate the angle by less than the thickness of a human hair, you will zoom past the moon

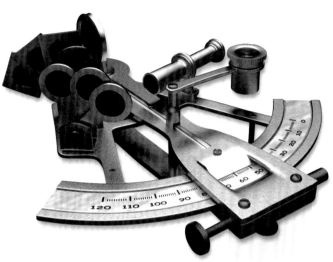

▲ Sextant

with no hope of turning around. You will drift to the outer reaches of the solar system and soon be dead.

With your sextant, you take five extremely precise readings to assist the computers down in Houston at Mission Control.

When they are satisfied with the results, your mind shifts back to the next and greatest danger you face during the time you will be orbiting Earth.

This seems fitting, too. Your kindred souls — those sailors of ancient times — faced the identical danger. The possibility that you will drown.

Because of this, you constantly monitor yourself for the signs of motion sickness. It is not that you are afraid of death but of how your death might be remembered.

43

After all, before strapping yourself into the capsule at sea level, more than 100 mi. (160 km) below, you had prepared yourself for the possibility of disaster at ignition or during the first few seconds of liftoff. You readied yourself again for the moment when the rocket faced maximum stress at Max-Q, far out of sight of the spectators on the ground.

At each of those three crucial points of danger, you knew that death would be instant and merciful. You would be mourned as a hero, remembered for eternity for your sacrifice and the work you did to prepare the way for others after you to walk on the moon.

Now, however, if something goes wrong before the last set of engines sends you hurtling at the moon, you will only blame yourself. If you fail to control your queasiness, your life and mission might face an inglorious ending. All because you gave in to the same weakness a 10-year-old might face on a roller coaster ride.

A small bolt floats in front of your space helmet. You are glad for a distraction to take you away from your queasiness. Someone must have misplaced it during construction.

That bolt is telling you that you are at zero gravity. You don't feel weightlessness, though. You are strapped in too tight.

You are in no hurry to unbuckle. Your reluctance comes from the fear of what might happen during the next two or three hours. When you are unbuckled, the slightest move can send you rolling in place like a ball. Zero gravity sounds like fun, but it's not a game. You've spent hours of training in the "Vomit Comet," a military

▼ Apollo 11 Mission Commander Neil Armstrong trains for the lunar landing, climbing the Lunar Module ladder in his space suit.

airplane that climbs at a steep angle, then levels and drops its nose. For about 25 seconds during this training, you are in free fall. You practiced the fall 60 times per session, and you have done dozens of sessions.

But still, you are afraid. You are wearing an airtight space helmet. The helmet is locked onto an airtight space suit. Your hands are in gloves and there is no way possible to reach back into your suit or helmet. You know what every flier in the Apollo program knows.

There are pills to prevent seasickness, but none for the effects of zero gravity. If you throw up from motion sickness in zero gravity, your vomit does not drop. Instead, it remains weightless in your helmet, where you will have no choice but to inhale it.

A sailor of ancient times would drown with his lungs filled with cold, salty water. If you give in to motion sickness, you would be remembered forever as the astronaut who suffocated on his own vomit.

You continue to fight the queasiness of zero gravity until 2 hours and 44 minutes after ignition. At this moment, with great relief, you hear Houston radio the words that will commit you fully to your epic and awesome journey: "You are GO for TLI." That's translunar injection. In other words, you have the green light to leave Earth's orbit and fly to the moon.

▲ Michael Collins all suited up

SOLVE THE TECHNOLOGY MYSTERY

It is October of 1707. While returning to England in bad weather, four warships of the British Royal Navy stray off course because the navigators miscalculated their longitude, or their east-west position. (The tool of the day — the sextant — is much better at measuring latitude, or north-south position.)

The four ships hit rocks off the Isles of Scilly and capsize. More than 1400 sailors lose their lives. Seven years later, the British government passes the *Longitude Act* and offers, in today's currency, nearly $4 million U.S. to anyone who can invent a device to accurately measure global position going east to west or west to east.

The future of human exploration — including the epic journey to the moon — depends on your solution to the problem.

Who are you, and what was your solution?

Answer at end of the chapter.

Isaac Newton.
Later, Sir Isaac Newton.

Before he was knighted and the world recognized him for his genius, most who knew Isaac Newton had good reason to think he was crazy. After all, wondering if changing the shape of his eyeball would distort his vision, he once took a long needle and poked it under the skin between his eyeball and the bone of his skull. Then he rubbed the needle around to see if anything happened. By good fortune, he didn't cut any important nerves. (Not that anyone knew what a nerve was then, anyhow.)

Newton's day job was as a mathematics professor at Cambridge University. Long before, as a student, he had wanted to

▲ Isaac Newton

know things that the tools of mathematics weren't good enough to help him figure out. So he decided to pursue an entirely new field in mathematics, called calculus. He kept calculus a secret for 27 years — mainly because he was distracted so easily. There were days when he would put his feet on the floor to get out of bed and then sit there for hours, lost in thought, forgetting he was supposed to go somewhere.

In August of 1684, one of the world's most famous astronomers of his time — Edmond Halley of Halley's Comet fame — stopped by to ask if Newton could suggest why planets orbit the way they do. And more important, Halley wanted to know if mathematicians could calculate the curve of planets as they circle the sun.

This was a very important question for the epic journey to the moon. Mathematicians would need Newton's answer to make sure the space capsule and the moon arrive at the same place in space at the same time. After all, the moon is zipping in orbit at 2288 mi. (3682 km) per hour, and the space capsule needs to travel 250 000 mi. (400 000 km) away from Earth to reach it. That's like hitting a moving baseball 100 mi. (160 km) away with a bullet. If the space capsule misses the moon, there won't be enough fuel to slow, stop, turn around and chase it.

Halley was astounded to learn that Newton already knew the answer. Newton had solved it one day when he was bored, but hadn't bothered to tell anyone.

Halley was even more astounded to learn that Newton couldn't find the mathematical solution he'd scratched out

among his many and scattered papers. This, in essence, was like having a formula for the cure to a deadly disease, but forgetting where you left it.

Halley asked Newton to redo the calculations on another piece of paper. It took Newton two years. Not because the mathematics was difficult, but because he became sidetracked by a bigger question.

When he finished answering the bigger question, Newton produced his masterwork and gave it a boring title: *The Mathematical Principles of Natural Philosophy*.

▲ A photo of Halley's Comet in 1986 (left); a 1910 illustration of the comet in 1682

> # Newton's first law described how "for every natural action, there is an equal and opposite reaction."

For the rest of the world, it was such a stunning achievement that it alone was greater than all of the previous mathematical discoveries in history.

Newton's first law described how "for every natural action, there is an equal and opposite reaction." His masterwork described the mathematics and the three laws required to make sense of all motions throughout the universe. Newton also gave future mathematicians the tools to calculate how to aim a space capsule to be in the exact right place at the exact right time to reach the moon.

Newton's three laws of motion were a huge step in the amazing and epic journey to the moon. (The other two laws were "objects at motion tend to stay in motion and objects at rest tend to stay at rest" and "force equals mass times acceleration.")

Still, Newton was wrong when he said that gravity was a force that attracted one object to another. Newton also had a few little details wrong about some other major things — like time and space.

It would take two and a half centuries for someone to change those views — someone who is often first remembered as a dunce. You'll meet him after you manage to get enough speed to escape the clutch of Earth's orbit.

STAGE THREE: THE BRAVEST MAN OF ANY APOLLO MISSION

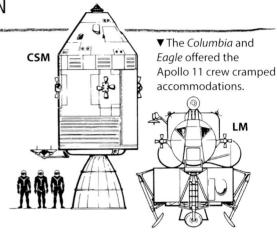

▼ The *Columbia* and *Eagle* offered the Apollo 11 crew cramped accommodations.

When you see a cartoon of a single-stage rocket shaped like a bullet with fins, it seems like a logical way to travel through space. But for the Apollo 11 program to succeed, the rocket design team needed to think of alternatives that weren't so seemingly obvious.

To begin with, this simplistic design has to face the simple facts of gravity. It takes 198 lb. (90 kg) of rocket fuel for every 1 lb. (0.5 kg) of equipment needed to reach orbit. A single-stage rocket with crew and equipment and life support would need far too much fuel to be practical.

Even if it were able to get to the moon, the logistics of landing a massive ship upright on its tail were next to impossible.

One of the first proposed solutions was called the Earth Orbit Rendezvous (EOR). EOR would send 15 smaller rockets into orbit around Earth. These would then be assembled into a larger vehicle to go to the moon and back.

While this avoided the problem of launching a monstrous rocket, EOR didn't solve the difficulty of landing it on its tail on the moon.

The alternate proposal was a Lunar Orbit Rendezvous (LOR), where smaller space capsules would be split and then later re-assembled at the moon. At first, most of the engineers were passionate in their hatred of the LOR idea. If something went wrong during orbit assembly around Earth, it would be relatively easy to bring the astronauts home. But if something went wrong in assembling a spacecraft out in lunar orbit, the astronauts would almost certainly be stranded and die slow, horrible deaths.

In the meantime, the space race was tightening between the United States and Russia. Under pressure, the engineers decided they had no choice but to make the LOR work.

The solution, then, was to chop the *Saturn V* rocket into stages that would fall away after use. The first two stages carried the bulk of the rocket fuel and did most of the work to thrust the payload into orbit around the Earth. The third stage carried the *Columbia* and the *Eagle* — the Command and Service Module (CSM) and the Lunar Module (LM).

This solution, however, was tricky. It required that first the CSM and LM needed to be connected in outer space during the orbit around Earth. Then, they had to be disconnected in lunar orbit for the moon landing and reconnected again after blasting off the moon.

In the end, of course, it was decided that this was the best method for success of Apollo 11.

But it did mean cramped living spaces. From July 16 to July 24, three grown men lived in a space smaller than the average bedroom — and not an empty bedroom, but one crammed with equipment everywhere, including the bulky space suits the astronauts were wearing. Given the lack of space and the bad food —

basically a mixture of freeze-dried paste and water — it's been described as the world's worst camping trip. But in this case, the campers can't even leave the tent. The astronauts had to stay inside the entire time, where they lived, cooked, ate and handled various body functions, such as expelling liquid and solid waste — and gas.

One downside to the horrible food that probably wasn't discussed by engineers during the design stage was digestion — more specifically, the gas it produced. It was so bad Buzz Aldrin later joked that they didn't really need the rocket engines because they could have produced enough thrust by themselves.

Eight days, three men, one small space, no showers and lots of body gas.

The situation led to an often-repeated statement by those who understood this reality of space travel: the bravest man of any Apollo mission was the Navy frogman sent to open the module's hatch after it splashed down at the end of the journey.

▲ After splashdown in the Pacific Ocean, the Apollo 11 astronauts wait in a life raft as a Navy frogman closes the capsule hatch.

Technology Mystery Solved

Congratulations, John Harrison!

You are self-educated as a carpenter and clockmaker and, against all odds, you came up with a solution to the longitudinal mystery.

The sextant already exists, and indeed will be an important part of the future moon journey. You know that once the sextant gives a navigator a latitude measurement, longitude can be calculated based on what time it is at zero degrees longitude, which was the location of the Royal Observatory in Greenwich, London.

What you need, then, is a mechanical clock that will run accurately no matter what the temperature or humidity or pressure is. The clock must also be so self-contained that a ship's movement won't affect it.

Most educated people of your day consider a technological feat like this to be impossible. You don't.

In 1772, you present King George III with a "sea watch" that after 10 weeks of testing is accurate to within one-third of one second per day. Yes, in 1772. It took you some four decades of tinkering, but you proved to the world it could be done. You changed navigation forever; no longer did ships get lost while at sea. Nor will future astronauts when they return to Earth to land in the Pacific Ocean.

EPISODE FIVE

AN INFINITE OCEAN OF SPACE

"This is Apollo Control. We are 10 minutes away from ignition on translunar injection. We want to add 10 435 feet per second to the spacecraft's velocity, looking for a total velocity at the end of this burn of about 35 575 feet per second."

— *NASA transcript, Apollo 11 mission*

◄ View of Earth showing clouds over water from the Apollo 11 spacecraft following translunar injection

STAGE ONE: TRANSLUNAR INJECTION

"You are a GO for TLI."

At 2 hours and 44 minutes after liftoff, these words from Houston have given you clearance for translunar injection.

Now you have a problem that you know will gradually worsen until you are in a position to fix it, and you can't help thinking about it. In the vacuum of space, there are no molecules of oxygen or nitrogen to maintain an even temperature.

The side of your capsule that faces the sun will get hot enough to boil your fuel tanks. On the other side, it will get cold enough to freeze the radiators solid.

This adds some urgency to completing the next stage of your journey.

Translunar injection means that you need to boost your speed again. Without that boost, you'll simply circle Earth for the years it would take for your orbit to decay and turn you into a meteor plunging to the planet.

To solve this, the engineers have designed stage three of your *Saturn V* rocket so it has one final ignition. It fired once earlier to get you into orbit, and then it shut down. Now it will fire again for 5 minutes and 47 seconds to power your final escape from Earth's gravity.

The fuel that will fire the third stage of your rocket is liquid oxygen, stored at −292°F (−180°C), and liquid nitrogen, at −423°F (−253°C). Place your hands in these liquids and your bones would shatter instantly.

Ignition of the two liquids, however, will produce a burn of over 3990°F (2200°C) and a new burst of acceleration.

▼ The massive third stage (S-IVB) of the *Saturn V* was powered by a single engine capable of almost 200 000 lb. (900 000 N) of thrust.

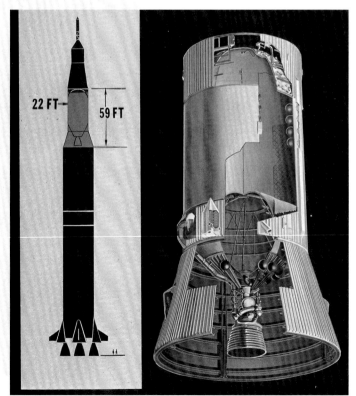

22 FT — 59 FT

You feel the push of that thrust for almost six minutes, until you have reached a speed of just under 25 000 mi. (40 235 km) per hour. That's fast enough to drive a car from Los Angeles to New York in the time it takes to drink a cup of coffee. It's enough speed to circle Earth at the equator in 60 minutes.

When the rocket engine shuts down, you are pointed at the emptiness of the solar system, with no more stage-three fuel to alter your speed or your path, moving at 10 times the speed of a bullet fired from a rifle. In the frictionless vacuum of outer space, you will drift at that speed to meet the moon at the precise time and location given to you by mathematics.

But you are still attached to stage three of the *Saturn V* rocket, which means things are about to get complicated. Very complicated. Stage one and stage two were rocket engines beneath what were essentially hollow tubes filled with fuel. Those stages fell away as the fuel was burned. Stage three is designed as a rocket engine and fuel, but it also contains the Lunar Module (LM), which you know as the *Eagle*.

Until now, you've merely been a passenger. Now the mission depends on you to complete some tricky flying of your own.

It's too late to turn around if you fail. What's ahead of you has been compared to driving an aircraft carrier with an outboard motor.

This is the situation. You are in the Command Module (CM), which is where you will live as you travel to the moon and back. You think of it as the *Columbia*. This cabin, covered in silver foil, will be the only part to return to Earth.

▲ The Apollo 11 Command and Service Module is ready to be mated with the Lunar Module adapter of the third stage.

53

▲ Joseph Shea helped persuade scientists at NASA that a Lunar Orbit Rendezvous (LOR) would work, using models to demonstrate how the Lunar Module would dock with the Command and Service Module.

The *Columbia*, however, needs a Service Module (SM) attached to it. It is your life support. The SM has fuel for propulsion, and it has your electrical power, your oxygen and your water. Together, these are called the Command and Service Module — the CSM.

Again, your journey is similar to that of the sailors of old. Just as a large ship can't go into shallow waters, you can't land on the moon with the *Columbia*. You need a smaller rowboat to take you to shore. For you, the rowboat is the Lunar Module, called the *Eagle*.

Once you reach the moon, you will transfer into the *Eagle*. The *Eagle* has two stages. Its lower stage will land you on the moon. You will leave the lower stage behind so that the upper stage can take you back to the *Columbia*.

That, however, is nearly three days away, but to get there, you need to successfully connect the *Columbia* and the *Eagle*. For now, your "rowboat to the moon" is still inside the third stage of the *Saturn V* rocket.

Moving away from Earth at this incredible speed, you fire up the thruster engines of the *Columbia*. You need to use a combination of help from computers and the

controls in front of you. In the years to come, virtual reality will be able to recreate the moment you are now facing. But that is not something you can imagine now.

On your left, you have a dashboard stick. You can twist it left or right, move it up or down, or push it in and out. A controller to your right comes out of the floor — it's a combination of stick and pedal. You've spent hours training to master these controls.

You delicately use the thrusters to detach from the third stage of the *Saturn V* rocket and briefly leave behind the Lunar Module. Here is the crucial moment. Mess up with the controls and you might spin away, never to return. Or worse, you might collide hard enough to crack open your capsule.

For that reason, all three of you remain in your space suits. You are fully aware of what happened during the Gemini 8 mission, when the first docking of two spacecraft in orbit was attempted. Yes. It failed and the astronauts found themselves in a spacecraft that was tumbling end over end. It was only the pilots' manual flight skills that allowed them to survive. The pilot? The same one now attempting this docking maneuver — Neil Armstrong.

Using both hands and the foot pedal, you fly the *Columbia* as it eases away from the third stage of the *Saturn V*. Slowly. Very, very slowly. You don't dare move more than 1 mi. (1.6 km) per hour faster than the rocket behind you.

Finally, you are clear, facing away from the rocket that brought you this far. But now you have to flip the *Columbia* around so that you are facing toward it.

As you do this slow-motion ballet in the weightlessness of space, you see the doors at the front open like flower petals. It reveals the *Eagle* inside the *Saturn V,* looking like a mechanical spider.

At the front of the *Columbia* is a probe — a tripod with a ball at the tip.

At the front of the *Eagle* is a drogue — a dish with a hole in the center. You need to guide the ball of the *Columbia*'s probe into the dish of the *Eagle* and click it into place.

All of these pieces are traveling in a dance at thousands of miles per hour, slingshotting away from Earth. Yet as you fire thrusters to head back to the third stage of the *Saturn V,* you need to keep the difference in speed between the *Columbia* and *Eagle* to less than a gentle bump.

Using the crosshairs of a scope, you breathe a sigh of relief as you hear the probe click into the hole in the center of the *Eagle*'s drogue plate. You trigger a shot of nitrogen gas that yanks some clamps into place, and now the *Columbia* and *Eagle* are connected by a tunnel big enough to crawl through.

You throw a switch to disconnect the *Columbia* and *Eagle* from the third stage of the *Saturn V* rocket. It falls away from you and becomes an empty shell that will orbit the sun for as long as the solar system exists.

Once you have connected wires so the *Eagle* receives electricity from the *Columbia,* you can finally remove your space suit.

Yet, for now, there is still that one last problem to solve.

On one side, the fuel tanks are getting hotter and hotter. On the other, your radiators begin to freeze.

So you turn sideways to the sun and use the thrusters to slowly spin, much like roasting a chicken over a barbecue.

And then you settle in for nearly three days of coasting through the solar system. Ahead of you is the infinite ocean of the universe, and you need to find and land on the speck of an island that we call the moon.

▼ The Command and Service Modules for the Apollo 11 and Apollo 12 missions meet in the Manned Spacecraft Operations Building at the Kennedy Space Center.

Solve the Engineering Mystery

You are an English scientist. It is 1831. You have coils of wire and a magnet. Something strange happens when you move the magnet through the coil. Little do you know that you are about to solve a problem crucial to the epic journey to the moon because astronauts will need electrical power inside their space capsule.

Who are you, and what did you learn that made the journey possible?

Answer at end of the chapter.

STAGE TWO: A DUNCE WHO WASN'T A DUNCE

The story's been told again and again that Albert Einstein was a dunce who flunked school and his teachers said he wouldn't amount to anything. While he was eccentric and hated wearing socks, it's not quite true that he was a dunce who later flourished.

A young Albert Einstein

The truth is he had no interest in memorizing facts to repeat them back like a parrot, and he had little interest in what the teachers wanted him to learn.

What he did enjoy, however, were what he called *Gedankenexperiments* — German for "thought experiments."

He imagined being a person standing on a moving train, at the midpoint of the train, as a friend outside watches the train pass from the platform. The friend sees lightning strike both ends of the train at the same time. But since the person on the train is moving toward one of those bolts of lightning, he would see that

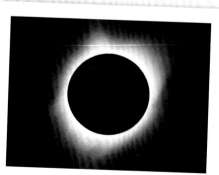

▲ A total solar eclipse

bolt first because its light has less distance to travel. From this observation, Einstein concluded that time and space are not the same for each person. It depends on where you are and how fast you are moving.

And what would happen, he wondered, if you could somehow chase a beam of light and catch up to it? You'd see that beam of light frozen in space. But since light would cease to be light if it were frozen, no matter how fast you went, it would always move away from you at the speed of light. This led Einstein to decide that time itself would change. If you could ever reach the speed of light, time would stop for you. And one other thing — your own mass would become infinite. His conclusion: motion changes time and space.

He also wondered what it would be like if you were floating in a box with no windows and suddenly the floor rose up to meet you. Is the box being pulled down by gravity or yanked upward by a rope? Conclusion: since you can't tell the difference, he decided gravity and acceleration were the same thing.

To Einstein, those conclusions meant something even more mind-boggling: gravity can affect time and space. So something as big as the sun will bend space and slow down time. The closer you are to a big mass that produces gravity, the more that time slows.

That contradicts the way we experience our own world. It seems so bizarre as to be impossible.

Yet in 1919, when the sun was photographed during a solar eclipse, scientists were able to show that the position of a star behind the sun was just an illusion. It was actually in a different place, but the gravity of the sun bent the light coming from that star.

Later, another experiment with atomic clocks, which are incredibly accurate down to millionths of a second, showed that a clock flown in a jet at high speed showed less elapsed time than a matching clock that remained on the ground.

Einstein came up with the math to show exactly how matter — like the mass of the sun — curved the space, and how curved space affected the matter within it. He explained his novel ideas about motion and gravity and space and time in his theory of general relativity.

There was one problem, however. It seemed that the law of the conservation of energy, a major scientific principle, was in conflict with his theory. (The law of the conservation of energy says that the total energy of a system stays the same over time.) Happily, though, Einstein had help from another genius mathematician, Emmy Noether. Noether provided a solution to Einstein's problem with her own theorem, which explained how symmetry in space was linked to conservation of energy.

Although the first part of her career was unpaid, and her work was given secondary status because she was a woman and because she was also Jewish, Noether finally gained recognition for her work. "Fraulein Noether was the most significant creative mathematical genius thus far produced since the higher education of women began," Einstein wrote.

Conflict resolved, the theory of relativity provided much-needed science for the Apollo 11 mission. Without this knowledge, our global positioning systems — GPS — would fail us, and make travel through space much less predictable. Gravity on Earth is stronger than gravity for the GPS satellites in orbit around Earth. Time literally moves slower for those satellites — not by much — but thanks to Einstein, and Noether, we are able to predict and measure those changes to ensure constant GPS accuracy.

His thought experiments and staggering genius, however, would have mattered little unless someone found a way to get past all the obstacles in the way of an object leaving Earth's gravity.

That took the birth of a boy born in a small town in Poland in 1912. A boy who, like Einstein, struggled with math and physics, at least in his teachers' eyes. Yet he believed he could build a rocket big enough to burst through the bubble of air that protects our planet.

Emmy Noether

STAGE THREE: ASTEROIDS, METEOROIDS, METEORS AND METEORITES

Good news: you'll never have to worry about Earth getting hit by a giant meteor.

Bad news: that's because most of us are using the wrong term. A meteor is what we commonly call a shooting star. A meteor is the trail of light that results when an asteroid enters Earth's atmosphere and burns because of the friction caused by its speed in the air. So it's actually the asteroid that will do damage, not the meteor. (Asteroids are rocky bodies that orbit the sun to occasionally intersect Earth's orbit, and a big batch of them is drifting between Mars and Jupiter.)

Good news: you shouldn't worry too much about a world-ending collision between Earth and a large object from outer space. Mainly, Earth takes hits from meteoroids, defined as small particles from a comet or asteroid. The vast bulk of meteoroids are about the size of a grain of sand. Day by day, about 200 000 lb. (90 700 kg) of meteoroids vaporize against our bubble of protective atmosphere. Maybe once a year, a meteoroid the size of a car hits our atmosphere, but burns up before it hits the ground, causing a spectacular light show as it dies in a blaze of glory. In fact, it takes a rock the size of three combined classrooms to manage to survive the intense friction against air, reaching impact at a vastly reduced size.

Bad news: while meteors are fun to watch, the real worry should be about meteorites — the term for the part of an asteroid big enough to survive the burn through the atmosphere and reach the ground. These can cause some serious damage. One meteoroid — which is what the object is called as it moves through the solar system — was about the size of a gymnasium

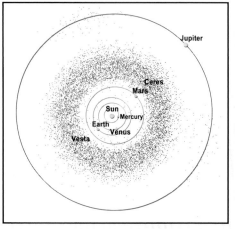

▲ An artist's illustration of the asteroid belt, from NASA's Dawn Mission Art series

when it entered the atmosphere. As a meteor, it burned down to a core no larger than a cantaloupe, and as a meteorite, at impact, it crashed through the roof and then through the floor of a house near Chicago, Illinois, to finally settle in a pile of laundry in the basement. That was in 2003.

The meteorite that is believed to have ended the dinosaur age was almost 6 mi. (10 km) wide at impact and caused a crater 112 mi. (180 km) wide. The explosion and debris altered the climate so badly that roughly three-quarters of all life on Earth was destroyed in the years that followed. (While this was bad news for dinosaurs, it wasn't so bad for the mammals that survived and eventually took over the space they had occupied.)

Good news: asteroids big enough to turn into meteorites large enough to threaten civilization only come along millions of years apart.

Bad news: when the next one hits, it won't be taking out dinosaurs.

Good news: now you understand all the terms that astronauts use when talking about the danger of collisions in outer space:

ASTEROID — rocky body in orbit around the sun

METEOROID — piece of asteroid or comet moving through outer space that causes a meteor

METEOR — the light from a burning meteoroid caused by friction as it enters the atmosphere

METEORITE — the core of an asteroid or comet that impacts the ground after creating a meteor during its burn through the atmosphere

▲ This photo of asteroid 243 Ida and its newly discovered moon was transmitted to Earth from NASA's *Galileo* spacecraft.

ENGINEERING MYSTERY SOLVED

Congratulations, Michael Faraday!

Although you had very little formal education, your work in understanding the nature of electromagnetism makes you one of the most influential scientists ever.

You have learned that passing a magnet through stationary wires or passing wires over a stationary magnet produces electricity. You will go on to construct an electric dynamo, leading future engineers to build electric motors, which are so crucial to the journey to the moon. Oh, and you will also outline the principles of the nature of electricity. When you proposed that electromagnetic forces extend into empty space around conductors, however, your ideas were rejected by the scientific community.

After your death, you will be proven correct. Because of this concept, you laid the foundation for all electromechanical devices so crucial to industry and to future spaceflight, including the *Columbia* spacecraft about to cross 200 000 mi. (322 000 km) of outer space.

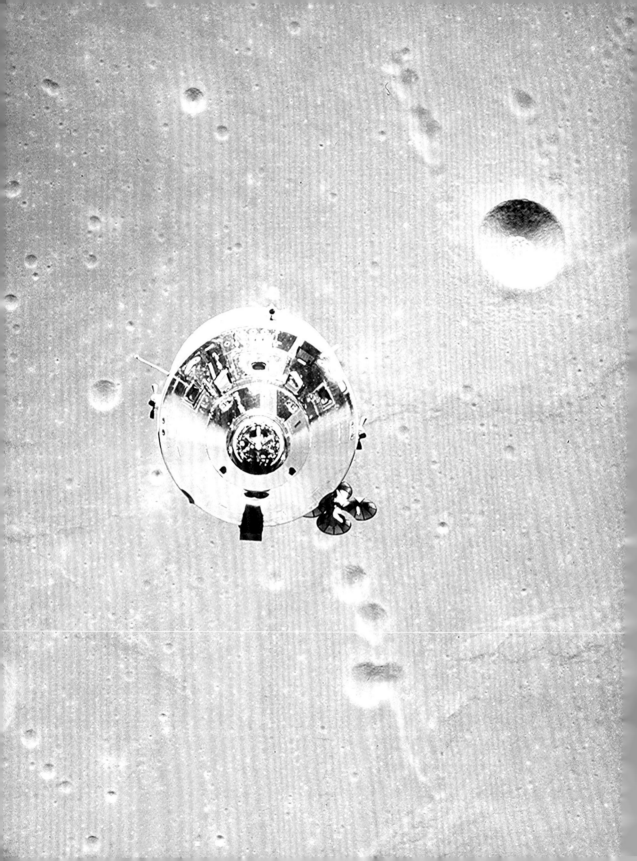

EPISODE SIX

SAILORS OF THE SOLAR SYSTEM

"This is Apollo Control at 5 hours, 11 minutes into the mission. The S4B slingshot maneuver was completed about 5 minutes ago. Designed to put the third stage of the launch vehicle into a trajectory that will take it behind the trailing edge of the moon and then into a solar orbit."

— *NASA transcript, Apollo 11 mission*

◀ A view of the *Columbia* from the *Eagle* in lunar orbit on July 20, 1969

Stage One: Absolute Zero

In your tiny silver ship, you are now like a sailor of ancient times. You have traded the heaving waters of Earth for a vast black ocean of space.

With no landmarks, you have no sensation of movement. Earth recedes too slowly to notice, and the moon only gets fractionally bigger each hour.

You can't feel it, but Earth's gravity tries to drag you back, and you've gradually been slowing down because of it. Still weak, but growing stronger, the moon's gravity pulls at you. And at the center of it all, some 93 000 000 mi. (149 669 000 km)

away and holding together all of the planets and asteroids of the entire solar system, the massive sun grips you and the moon and the Earth, curving the path of each.

At some point, your angle changes and you discover that you will miss your target unless you take precise and controlled action. For three crucial seconds of your journey, then, you ignite the *Columbia*'s rocket to adjust your course. For three crucial seconds, your tiny silver ship flares defiance against gravity, like a sailor of old lighting a lantern in the face of a hurricane.

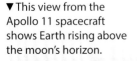
▼ This view from the Apollo 11 spacecraft shows Earth rising above the moon's horizon.

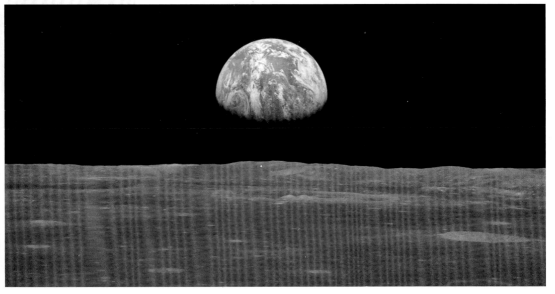

NEAR DISASTER AT LUNAR IMPACT	FIRST FOOTSTEP	MOONWALK	STRANDED FOREVER?	THE BIG BURN	JOURNEY'S END

That adjustment puts you back on course, protected by a life support system that gives you oxygen and provides water and heat. Only this system and the skin of your spacecraft protect you from a terrifying temperature of −455°F (−270°C). This is just short of absolute zero, where all molecules and atoms essentially cease to move.

Sailors in ancient times awaiting landfall swabbed the decks. You clean.

You purge fuel cells. You recharge batteries. You dump wastewater and watch it form spectacular crystals outside your window as it turns to ice. You check chlorine levels in the drinking water.

And you replace the filters that pull carbon dioxide out of the air. This is important. On Earth, a scuba diver uses a tank of air in an hour. Here, because you remove the carbon dioxide, you are able to inhale the same air with more efficiency and use all available oxygen, and you make a tank last 15 hours.

And you eat. You squeeze ham sandwich spread out of a tube. Or tuna. Or chicken salad. You add hot water to freeze-dried roast beef and vegetables, then mash it in its tube to make a mush that you squeeze into your mouth like toothpaste.

DATE FRUIT CAKE

BEEF SANDWICHES

CHEESE SANDWICHES

STRAWBERRY CUBES

▲ Space food in 1969

And you relieve yourself. Although not like a sailor, over the side of the ship. In zero gravity, this is no easy task. You use a tube with a vacuum, turning a valve that draws in your urine. Any leaks become tiny amber bubbles that float across the cabin. Pooping means unrolling a bag with tape on the edges. The bag tapes on to your skin. You make your deposit carefully, knowing that nothing goes to the bottom of the bag. You have to make sure you've collected everything before pulling the tape and the bag away from your skin.

Like a sailor of ancient times, you sleep.

You draw the window shades to block the blinding sun. You dim the cabin lights. You float in a mesh hammock shaped like a sleeping back. It is tethered to keep you from knocking into the dash or another astronaut.

▲ A view from the Apollo 11 spacecraft of the Crater Daedalus on the far side of the moon

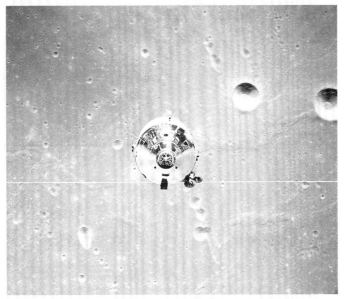

▲ From the *Eagle* in orbit above, a chance to photograph the *Columbia* with the moon's Sea of Fertility as a background

You will never feel sleep this luxurious again. In zero gravity, there are no pressure points, no awareness of anything except sweet slumber.

You gaze at the stars. But because of the unfiltered sunlight that fills the *Columbia*, the pupils of your eyes have narrowed so much that you can see only bright objects. If you want to see the stars gradually appear, you have to block out the sun and wait minutes for your eyes to adjust. With any flash of sunlight, the stars disappear again.

And you turn your eyes to the moon. Again and again.

You remember the moon as it appeared to you when you were a child, and you dreamed of being an astronaut. A flat gray disk in the sky.

Wondrous then. But infinitely more wondrous now as it begins to fill more and more of the largest window of the *Columbia*, until it seems you can reach out and touch it.

The moon is now between you and the sun. It creates a halo. What is special is that the surface of the moon is lit by earthshine — light from the sun bouncing off the planet. In the bluish glow of this light, you see large craters and dark flat areas. You see the scars of billions of years of meteorite impacts.

Almost reluctantly, you turn back to your tasks.

If you don't slow down, you'll shoot past the moon and out into the reaches of the solar system, never to return.

You fire up the *Columbia*'s rocket engine again. This time, not for three seconds, but for more than six minutes. And when you've slowed your pace enough, the moon's gravity pulls you into its orbit.

You skim above the moon now, only 62 mi. (100 km) from its surface. Only a handful of humans have been given this profound experience — the astronauts of Apollo 8, Apollo 9 and Apollo 10. They were the pioneers who proved that all of the steps along the way were possible.

You shiver with fear … and excitement, wonder and gratitude. Because unlike any human before you, your mission is to step onto the moon.

Incredibly, however, your vehicle is not the only vehicle on track to reach the moon.

Three days before liftoff, the Soviets sent their own spaceship.

▼ Astronaut Michael Collins in a Command Module simulator. He is at the docking tunnel, which provides passageway to and from the Lunar Module after docking.

Solve the Engineering Mystery

You are a Swiss engineer. It is 1941 and you are hiking and hunting with your dog, an Irish setter with long, silky fur. On your return, you discover that your pants and your dog's fur are covered in pesky burrs.

Instead of feeling the irritation that most would feel with all the work ahead of removing those burrs, you are curious.

How, you wonder, is it that the burrs stick the way that they do? When you find the answer, you also solve one of the problems of space travel — how to keep objects in place in zero gravity.

Who are you, and what does your discovery spur you to do?

Answer at end of the chapter.

STAGE TWO: THE ROCKET SCIENTIST WHO BELIEVED IN SCIENCE FICTION

Although he later had to flee Hitler, Wernher von Braun — inventor of the *Saturn V* rockets used in the Apollo space program — owed his life to the German dictator of World War II.

Von Braun was a scientist, born into German royalty, who once dreamed of being a composer. His passion for science began when, as a boy, he received a telescope and developed a love for astronomy. One of his early experiments almost caused a riot in Berlin after he attached fireworks to his toy wagon and lit the fuse on a crowded street.

He had failing math and physics marks in school until reading science fiction convinced him that it was possible for humans to fly through outer space. Then he forced himself to study both subjects until he was good enough to teach them to others. Understanding the science of physics, he realized, was crucial to building rockets that could escape the gravity of Earth.

As a university student, he had written a paper on rocket engines that drew the attention — and research money — from the German army. This was 14 years before his arrest.

While he was using his exacting approach to building rockets, he held on to a boyhood pleasure, even though it was a crime under Hitler's dictatorship. Using a false name and diplomatic pouches, he smuggled into Germany copies of a magazine called *Astounding Science Fiction*.

It was another crime, however, that led von Braun to his arrest late in World War II by the dreaded German secret police known as the Gestapo. His crime? As someone who dreamed of turning science fiction into science reality, he did not want his team's V-2 rockets to land on the wrong planet: Earth.

Nazi Germany wanted to use his rockets to destroy

▲ Wernher von Braun in early July, 1969. He stands in front of the *Saturn V* as it is prepared for the Apollo 11 mission. The *Saturn V* was developed by the Marshall Space Flight Center under his direction.

London; von Braun wanted his rockets to fly to the moon. In February of 1944, the Gestapo arrested von Braun and he was charged with planning to escape to Britain to share his rocket science with the enemy. As he spent days in prison, he must have thought about how the Gestapo had tortured and executed prisoners for far less than this.

While von Braun waited to learn his fate, fellow rocket scientists appealed directly to Hitler, advising that the V-2 program would fail without von Braun. As a result, Hitler commanded that von Braun be released.

> In the early 1950s, in the magazine *Colliers*, von Braun shared his vision for a moon landing in what became one of the most popular series of science articles of all time.

Time would eventually reveal that the Gestapo accusations were correct, for it was von Braun who later led his team to escape Hitler at the end of World War II.

Ironically, once he'd made it to America, he soon found himself in the position of developing weapons for the United States military, which wanted missiles capable of crossing the oceans.

Again, von Braun looked for ways to defy the military and instead follow his dream. This time, he did it as publicly as possible. Advertising!

Early in the 1950s, in the magazine *Colliers*, von Braun shared his vision for a moon landing in what became one of the most popular series of science articles

of all time. Many historians say this was the real beginning of the U.S. space program.

From there, von Braun went on to run the Apollo program, the same program that put Armstrong and Aldrin on the moon in 1969.

But, as you'll learn after you've landed the *Eagle*, the trip wouldn't have been possible without another amazing rocket ship pioneer, this one an American named Robert Goddard.

▲ Jules Verne's first science fiction novel, *From the Earth to the Moon*, was published in 1865. As the illustration shows, Verne's spaceship passengers enjoy weightlessness.

STAGE THREE: THE FORMATION OF THE MOON

Science today doesn't give us a clear picture of how the moon became the moon. Blame for this uncertainty rests squarely on the astronauts of Apollo 11 and the others who walked on the moon during subsequent Apollo missions 12, 14, 15, 16 and 17.

Until they collected their moon rocks and brought them back to Earth, it was generally agreed that early in the solar system's history, a large object about the size of Mars hit Earth with a sideways blow.

Dynamics is the branch of mechanics that studies the effects of the forces of moving objects. Computer simulations showed how this long-ago collision would have spit out debris from both Earth and the impacting object. The debris spun into orbit and eventually collected

into a sphere that we call the moon. What's crucial about this theory is that dynamics show that most of what formed the moon would have come from the object that hit Earth, not Earth itself.

Yet lunar rocks show that the moon and Earth have similar ratios of key elements like titanium, calcium, oxygen and tungsten. It was an easy conclusion that one came from the other. So the material did not originate from a second object that hit Earth. Scratch that theory.

"Aha!" said some scientists who favored a newer theory to explain the similarity: a single giant impact is not how it happened. Instead, over a long period of time, when Earth was young and made of molten rock, it endured dozens of lesser impacts with smaller objects, each throwing out a spray of moonlets that eventually became compacted into the moon as we see it now.

New simulation dynamics show that, yes, this could be possible if there were 20 or more impacts with Earth. That would explain why lunar rocks are so similar to the composition of Earth.

Settled then.

Not so fast. Again, those pesky astronauts and their moon rocks.

This newer theory could only be true if the formation of the moon took place over the 100 million or so years it took for all these accidental smaller collisions.

Recent analysis of the moon rocks — using new techniques to reevaluate the age of the uranium in the rock — shows the moon to be about 4.5 billion years old, far too old to be formed by a series of small collisions that created moonlets.

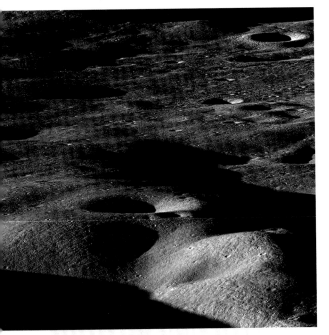

▲ On the moon, mountains are formed as a result of impacts.

Even worse for the moonlets theory, Apollo 14 brought back rocks with zircon grains that scientists presume were formed from a volcanic type of ocean right after the moon was formed. These grains could only exist if the moon was produced from the white-hot debris that remained after a single massive collision from something that hit Earth.

So, back to the original theory. But how to explain the similarity of the moon rocks to Earth?

Still, unfortunately, a mystery.

Worse still, now a different analysis of moon rocks shows that while the moon is extremely dry right now, it likely had a lot of water when it formed.

Explain that!

Nobody, it seems, has been able to do it so far.

Isn't it ironic that the act of landing on the moon has led us, in one way, to understanding less about the moon than we did before the landing?

▲ This moon rock, the first sample photographed in the Lunar Receiving Laboratory, is similar in composition and appearance to igneous rock types found on Earth.

ENGINEERINGMYSTERYSOLVED

Congratulations, George de Mestral!

By taking those burrs and examining them under a microscope, you have found something very interesting.

The burrs are covered with thousands of tiny hooks. These hooks will bind themselves to any fabric or hair. You decide that this could be a way to replace buttons. All you need to do is create tiny plastic hooks and attach them to a fuzzy fabric.

The idea sounds great, but it takes you nearly 20 years to find a way to manufacture this on a large scale. You are excited about the chance to take it to the marketplace and sell as much as you can.

But nobody really cares.

Until NASA saw it as a way to keep objects attached to walls in zero gravity. Then, suddenly, de Mestral's invention was space age and cool and used in all sorts of clothing, from running shoes to jackets to watch straps. As for the astronauts making the long and weightless journey to the moon, they'd depend on your invention, which becomes a household name after NASA sees the value in it.

The household name? That, too, was de Mestral's invention. He combined "velvet" for the soft fabric and "crochet" for the hooks, and came up with a single word. You guessed it: Velcro.

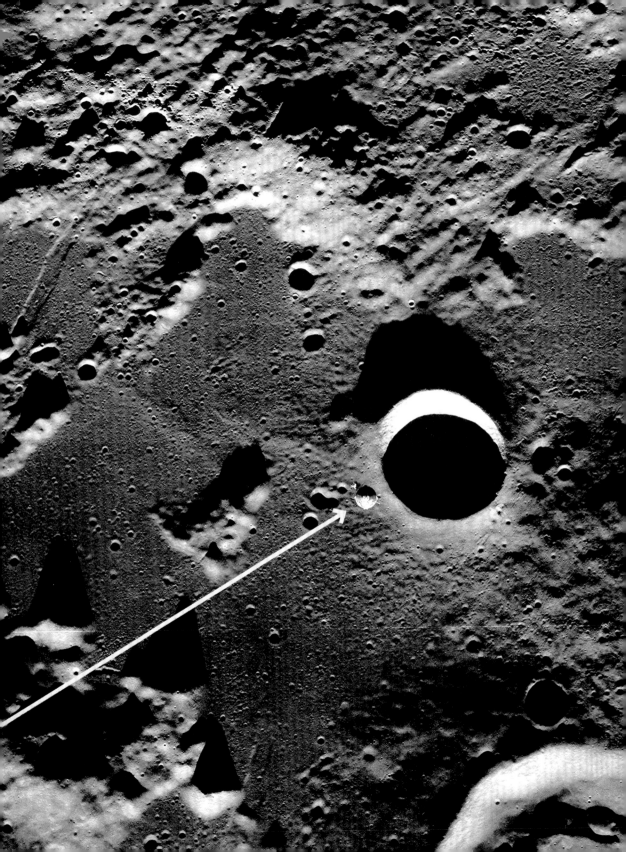

+100:39:00

HOUR   MINUTE   SECOND

EPISODE SEVEN

NEAR DISASTER AT LUNAR IMPACT

"And, Houston, we got a 500 alarm early in the program."

— *NASA transcript, Apollo 11 mission*

◄ The Apollo 11 Command and Service Module is the tiny dot beside the large crater in this view from the Lunar Module.

STAGE ONE: CODE 12-0-2!

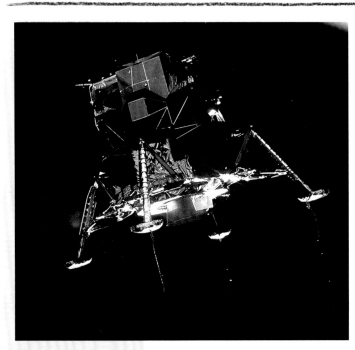

▲ The *Eagle* in landing configuration was photographed from the *Columbia*. The long rods under the landing pods are lunar surface sensing probes that, on contact, sent a signal to crew to shut down the descent engine.

It's day five and you've circled the moon 13 times, going from bright sunshine on one side to darkness on the other. Each orbit gives you another look at your intended landing area — the Sea of Tranquility.

It's the perfect place. Flat. Smooth.

You fight your excitement. There are still too many things that could go wrong between now and your first step on the moon. You or Mission Control might abort the mission at any of the stages along the way.

First, you need to disconnect from the mother ship, the *Columbia*. On board the *Columbia*, one of the three of you will remain behind to help when you are ready to return. You hear the click of the hatches separating, and you drift a short distance away in the *Eagle*.

You don't notice the unanticipated and troubling event that is occurring. You don't hear the tiny puff of air as it escapes from the chamber between the *Columbia* and the *Eagle*. Like a cork popping from a bottle, it adds the tiniest bit of speed to the *Eagle*. Soon, however, you'll discover exactly how that little puff might cost you your life.

You think all is well. Then, as nozzles spray two types of fuel into the thrust chamber of the *Eagle's* rocket engine, they ignite on contact.

In the *Eagle*, you use the rocket thrusters to slowly make a full turn so the *Columbia* can inspect the *Eagle* as you drift away. All sides of the *Eagle* need to be free of damage after the journey from Earth. All four legs of the landing gear need to be extended. Only a visual inspection from the *Columbia* will confirm the mission is a go.

You pass this first test. You are cleared to begin the final 62 mi. (100 km) of your journey to the surface of the moon and touch down with the fragile, bug-like legs of your Lunar Module.

You are dropping at more than 1 mi. (1.6 km) a second, but you don't feel it in zero gravity. At this speed, you will crash land in under a minute. You need precious rocket fuel to slow your speed so you can make a tiptoe landing on a safe, flat space among the huge and jagged rocks below.

You also need to make sure you land the *Eagle* upright on its four fragile legs. This is not an easy task. The *Eagle* is designed in two pieces. The lower half has rocket thrusters and fuel to land you. The upper half will detach and take you back to your mother ship. However, as the lower half burns its fuel during descent, the upper half will become increasingly top heavy with fuel.

You are grateful that all of this has been programmed for a computer-controlled touchdown.

Then it happens. The shrill sound of an alarm from the *Eagle's* on-board computer breaks your concentration as you are punching downward toward the moon at nearly 3007 mi. (4839 km) per hour.

Program alarm. Code 12-0-2. The computer has overloaded!

Your first reaction is to wait for a command to abort the mission. You don't know if you'd survive. It would mean flipping the *Eagle* end over end, and then exploding the two sections apart and hoping the thrusters can take you back into orbit.

The alarm keeps clanging. But you sense no panic from Mission Control. Nothing indicates anything wrong with the *Eagle* itself. Your on-board computer weighs 17½ lb. (8 kg), but only has a memory of 36 KB — much, much less than a cell phone will contain a generation later. Finally, and after much anguish, the engineers in Houston decide to gamble. Maybe the alarm has been triggered because so many performance signals are hitting the computer that it can't absorb them all. They go with that scenario.

You are still a go for landing.

At 25 000 ft. (7620 m) of altitude, the computer tilts the ship upright so it will land feet first. The computer begins to increase the thrust from 10 percent to 100 percent to make the final descent slow and smooth.

At 4002 ft. (1220 m) above the moon, you drop your speed to a mere 98 ft. (30 m) per second.

Another alarm goes crazy. Now you are at an altitude of only 3001 ft. (915 m), mere seconds away from the tricky landing.

▼ NASA sketches illustrate the steps between orbiting the moon and landing on it.

Transfer to LM

Separation of LM from CSM

Landing on Moon

73

The program alarm sounds again. But it's a different code.

The craters below seem to be growing wider and wider. You know the craters aren't actually expanding. Instead, it's your visual. You are still moving fast. Maybe too fast. The alarm keeps clanging.

You call back to Mission Control via radio. "Twelve alarm. Twelve-oh-one."

▼ This is the crater near the point on the moon where the *Eagle* touched down.

Seconds later you hear back. "Go! Just go!" You're too close to turn around. The decision is made. Another overload on the computer memory? That's another gamble. No one knows for sure.

Go! Just go!

If the engineers at Mission Control are wrong, you are only seconds away from a spectacular crash. You'll be the first humans on the moon. And its first fatalities.

The "Just go!" command turns out to be a good gamble. Later, you'll learn the problem was a result of an error in the checklist manual. The rendezvous radar switch was set in the wrong position, and the unnecessary data it was sending used up 15 percent more computer memory — asking the computer to work beyond its capacity.

Crisis resolved. But now …

You realize that everything so far has been like a stroll along a sunny beach compared to what's ahead — because now you notice you have overshot the safe landing zone. By 4 mi. (6.5 km)! This is the disaster that a tiny puff of air during separation has caused. No longer will the computer control a perfect landing on the moon's Sea of Tranquility. All you see ahead are boulders and craters. The boulders look as big as four-story buildings.

That means you have to pilot the *Eagle* yourself. Beyond the crater. How will you control any feelings of panic? You are forced to draw upon your years and years of experience in flying all sorts of aircraft through all types of near disasters. To control the *Eagle* itself, you draw upon endless hours of practice on Earth. But the moon has one-sixth the gravity of Earth and almost no atmosphere. No amount of practice feels like the real thing.

It all rests on you.

The low-fuel light goes on. Yes, you are almost out of fuel. You know that the moon has nearly zero atmosphere. You can't glide.

The *Eagle* is dropping like a piano. No time to abandon the lower half of the Lunar Module for the upper half that would take you back to orbit.

You are moving downward and across at 20 ft. (6 m) per second. You were wrong about the size of those boulders. You now see they are as large as football stadiums. Landing there is certain death.

Your fingers tighten, then ease the controls; tighten, then ease. You nudge your controls to use 16 positioning thrusters to rock and skid the *Eagle*. You are skimming over the surface at 9 ft. (2.75 m) per second. It's still too fast. If you don't make a level landing, you won't survive. It's that simple.

Then you see it. Beyond the crater and the boulders. A flat and smooth spot. You add more thrust, gulping precious fuel.

The astronaut beside you gives you vital information, reading out the drop in altitude. Five percent fuel remains. Only 90 seconds until the thrusters flame out. And that's only if the reading is accurate.

You continue to drop down and across. You haven't cleared the boulders. It looks like they are reaching up for you. You are now 295 ft. (90 m) from a crash landing, and the *Eagle* is dropping at 3 ft. (1 m) a second.

Now, with so little fuel, it's even more crucial you land exactly level. Above you, the top half of the Lunar Module is so heavy with fuel, the slightest tilt will topple your landing.

No chance to abort. There are four possibilities. You will run out of fuel and crash. You will hit the rocks. You will clear the rocks, land on a flat spot and flip over. Or you will set it down, level and slow, then remain upright and survive.

Then, with four seconds of fuel remaining — four seconds! — a contact light goes on. It confirms what you knew when you felt a slight bump. You have landed. Level.

This is what the world hears by radio, nearly 250 000 mi. (400 000 km) away, at 4:14 p.m., Eastern Standard Time, on Sunday, July 20: "Houston … the Eagle has landed."

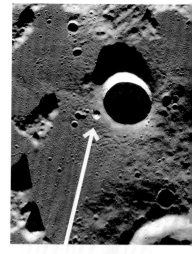

▲ From above, the Apollo 11 CSM is just a dot compared to some of the craters on the moon.

SOLVE THE TECHNOLOGY MYSTERY

It's one of the most crucial moments of the Apollo 11 mission. The Lunar Module is headed from orbit around the moon to land on the surface of the moon. But the Apollo Guidance Computer alarms begin to shriek.

Decision time. Go? No go? Go? No go?

With seconds to spare before it was too late to turn back in case of disaster, Houston engineers made their call: There is no problem. The only reason the alarms are going is that the computer is overloaded. Everything else is in order. Go!

The mystery is not why the on-board computer was overloaded. In fact, that very problem had been anticipated. Even with the best technology available at the time, there simply wasn't enough computing power available in a unit small enough to fit in the Lunar Module.

The mystery that needed solving was how to adapt this computer to all of the tasks it needed to handle for a successful moon landing.

Who are you, and how did you solve this problem?

Answer at end of the chapter.

STAGE TWO: TRY, TRY AGAIN

The headline read: "Moon rocket misses target by 238 799 ½ miles."

That summed up the story in a Worcester, Massachusetts, newspaper in 1929 shortly after a rocket failure by a local professor named Robert H. Goddard.

It was shortsighted and mean-spirited reporting. Three years earlier, this same professor had made rocket history with the first liquid-fueled flight. That rocket rose only 41 ft. (12.5 m), and curved sideways to land less than three seconds later only 184 ft. (56 m) away in a cabbage field.

Still, he had proven that liquid fuels could work as an alternative to powdered explosives. (The site is now a U.S. national historic landmark.) And his tests did not result in any fatalities, unlike the legendary first attempt at rocket flight in ancient China many centuries earlier.

According to the legend, the honor for that "flight" goes to a Wan Hu, a fictional minor Chinese official of the time. By then, the Chinese had devised tubes filled with gunpowder attached to arrows. One end of the tube would be capped and the other left open. When the powder was lit, the fire, gas and smoke produced thrust out of the open end. As weapons, these arrow rockets weren't accurate, but, fired in the thousands, they still did an effective job against the enemy.

Minor official or not, Wan Hu was still able to recruit many assistants to assemble a chair with two large kites. Fixed to these kites were 47 large arrow rockets.

▶ Wan Hu is a fictional Chinese official who was described in twentieth-century stories as the world's first "astronaut." The crater Wan-Hoo on the far side of the moon is named after him.

On the day of flight, Wan Hu sat in the chair. Upon his order, 47 assistants rushed forward with torches, lit one fuse each, then rushed away.

The result was predictable: a huge roar and billows of smoke. When it all cleared, Wan Hu and the flying chair were gone. Nobody really believes he flew anywhere. Fire arrows, after all, were just as likely to explode as to fly.

In the centuries that followed, however, gunpowder and various other dry explosives were the standard fuel for any rocket experiment. Goddard, too, began with gunpowder. But he ran tests to show that powder rockets only convert 2 percent of energy into thrust — something that the Chinese official Wan Hu could have verified all those centuries before, if only the other 98 percent of the energy had not torn him and his chair and kites into pieces too small to find.

Ahead of his historic first, albeit short, liquid-fueled rocket flight into a cabbage field, Goddard had proven three

> ## "Goddard's experiments in liquid fuel saved us years of work, and enabled us to perfect the V-2 years before it would have been possible."

▲ Robert Goddard was a theoretical scientist and practical engineer. He is known as the father of American rocketry.

crucial things that would eventually make Apollo 11 possible. The first was that liquid fuels are far more efficient than explosive powders. The second was that nozzles greatly increase thrust. And the third was that rockets would work in a vacuum, a notion that was at first mocked in the media. Common sense, after all, made it clear that rocket thrust needed something to push against, like an atmosphere.

When Goddard published a paper suggesting common sense was wrong and that, indeed, it was possible for a rocket to reach the moon someday, an editorial in the lofty *New York Times* heaped its share of media scorn upon him. It stated that Goddard "does not know the relation of action and reaction, and of the need to have something better than a vacuum against which to react … he only seems to lack the knowledge ladled out daily in high schools."

Goddard didn't quit. Instead, he merely stopped publicizing anything he did.

In 1945, Goddard was in an American naval laboratory when he saw one of Wernher von Braun's V-2 rockets for the first time. He was astounded at its similarities to his experimental rockets. Before World War II, the Germans had been aware of Goddard's work. As von Braun said years later, "Goddard's experiments in liquid fuel saved us years of work, and enabled us to perfect the V-2 years before it would have been possible."

And the snooty *New York Times*, which was proven so wrong by Goddard?

It finally did publish a correction to the editorial, which concluded with these words: "Further investigation and experimentation have confirmed the findings of Isaac Newton in the seventeenth century and it is now definitely established that a rocket can function in a vacuum as well as in an atmosphere. *The Times* regrets the error."

Perhaps if the correction had been offered shortly after the 1920 editorial, it might have meant something to Goddard.

But he'd been dead for over two decades by then. The *New York Times* did not publish its admission of regret until July 17, 1969 — a full day into Apollo 11's journey to the moon.

Stage Three: Preparing for Life after the Funeral

Of the hundreds of millions of people across the world who watched the unfolding drama of the Apollo 11 mission, three women undoubtedly felt the most stress. They were, of course, the wives of the astronauts — Janet Armstrong, Joan Archer (Aldrin) and Pat Collins.

Their children? Not so much. Instead of watching the mission on television, Mike Collins Jr. preferred playing with his pet bunny, Snowball. Young Marky Armstrong looked up once at the television and realized his dad was on the screen, so he ran over to hug it. None of the children really understood the risks their fathers were taking.

Their mothers, on the other hand, were understandably worried, because they realized the dangers their husbands faced. They also realized something else: how little life insurance their husbands carried.

It's a popular myth that Apollo astronauts were unable to get coverage. But in fact, the risk of dying was so great that life insurance was too expensive for them to purchase on their government salaries. In today's dollars, the life insurance policy would have costed $300 000. Worse, government regulations forbade NASA from purchasing the insurance for them.

While two private companies did pitch in to help with the insurance for the families of the Apollo 11 astronauts, the men themselves used another method to provide for their families if they never returned.

Postcards.

In the weeks before the mission, the astronauts signed hundreds of copies of a special postcard that commemorated the mission. While they were in the rockets on the day of the launch, a trusted friend would go to the Kennedy Space Center post office and get the stamps postmarked. The cards, however, would not be mailed, but left behind for the astronauts' families to sell if the astronauts died in space.

After all, the astronauts reasoned, that kind of tragic death would make those postcards extremely valuable.

The astronauts would also take other copies of the postcards on the mission, knowing that signed copies of these artifacts would also have a high value if they survived the mission.

Today, in collectors' circles, the postcards are known as "insurance covers" and "flown covers." It should be no surprise that there are only a limited number in existence.

You can still get one, if you'd like, since they occasionally show up at auctions across the world. You just need to be prepared to spend $20 000 to $45 000 to bring it home.

▲ A wreath-laying ceremony at Arlington National Cemetery is part of NASA's Day of Remembrance. Every January since 2004, wreathes are laid in memory of the men and women who lost their lives in the exploration of space.

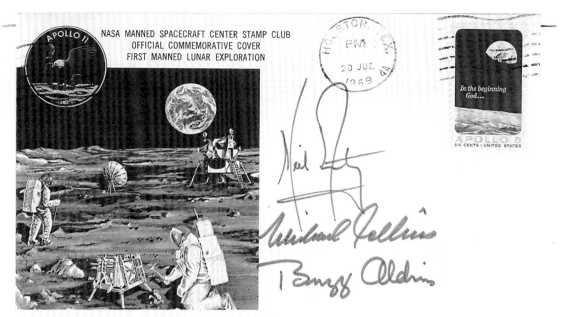

▲ The Apollo 11 astronauts signed "insurance covers" to provide for their families in case they didn't return to Earth.

TECHNOLOGY MYSTERY SOLVED

Congratulations, Margaret Hamilton!

You realized that if the Apollo Guidance Computer couldn't handle all the tasks, you needed to design the on-board flight software so that it would adapt to the anticipated overload.

As an American computer scientist and systems engineer, and team leader for development of in-flight software for the Apollo missions, you had the brilliant idea to treat the situation as if you were a physician in an emergency hospital room: focus first on the people with life-threatening injuries and let patients with lesser injuries wait till later.

You ensured that the software was programmed to set aside low-priority tasks and focus on crucial tasks first. You also incorporated a complete set of recovery programs into the software. And you built in a warning system to alert when there was an overload. If you had not found a way for the computer to overcome its hardware limitations, the Apollo 11 lunar landing would likely have either not occurred or ended in disaster.

You won the NASA Exceptional Space Act Award for this work, and recognition that the concepts you and your team created "became the building blocks for modern software engineering."

EPISODE EIGHT

FIRST FOOTSTEP

"We'll get to the details of what's around here, but it looks like a collection of just about every variety of shapes, angularities, granularities, every variety of rock you could find."

— *NASA transcript, Apollo 11 mission*

◄ Edwin "Buzz" Aldrin is walking on the moon. Neil Armstrong, who took the photograph, is reflected in Aldrin's helmet visor.

STAGE ONE: A CRUCIAL FOUR MINUTES

▲ Neil Armstrong prepares to put on his helmet with the help of a space-suit technician before leaving for Launch Pad 39A.

You and the *Eagle* are safely on the moon. You begin a new countdown. You have less than four minutes to decide if you can stay or if you need to abort the mission and launch back to the *Columbia*. Why? If you miss this four-minute window, you'll need to wait two hours for the *Columbia* to complete another orbit around the moon. If there is a system failure, that two hours might be fatal.

You don't realize that Mission Control is in a frenzy. Fuel has frozen and become plugged in a heat exchanger of the *Eagle*'s pipes. Temperature and pressure are rising. It might explode and topple the *Eagle* — or worse, destroy it.

They are about to ask you to "burp" the engine by flicking it on, then off. They hope that this will relieve the pressure. Then, just as they are set to tell you about the potential explosion, the ice plug disappears, and all is good.

For now.

As your heart rate settles from the near disaster at landing, you think of aliens — and not in a joking way, not when you are verging on the most momentous first step in human history. Four hundred years of science and technology have brought you to this moon landing. Four hundred thousand men and women are part of the team that brought you here. An estimated 530 million people across the world are watching this on television. You think back to Earth, which is now casting its bluish glow on the Sea of Tranquility.

Before the mission, engineers had decided that, unlikely as it was, there could be an alien encounter on the moon. So they designed the outer visor of your helmet not only to reflect the sun's blinding rays but to make it impossible for an alien to peer into a human face.

That's because it's their job to plan for any possibility. Your space suit needs to be able to withstand cosmic rays and solar radiation, and also micro-meteorites about the size of a marble. They have calculated there's a 1 in 10 000 chance that one might strike you, at 64 000 mi. (103 000 km) per hour.

To keep you alive, your Extravehicular Activity (EVA) suit has 500 parts and is three layers thick, with a fourth layer at every joint. It weighs 55 lb. (25 kg), not including the backpack that will pump oxygen and air conditioning. Like a scuba diver, you have to take your artificial world everywhere you go. Unlike a scuba diver, if your equipment fails, no amount of effort can bring you to an atmosphere where you can survive. This suit is literally your life.

Getting into these space suits will take you and your crewmate three hours each. Inside the *Eagle*, it will be like two football players putting on full equipment as they share a room the size of a closet.

You begin with your diaper and a waist-bag urinal system. Next, the cotton long johns, with a network of thin, water-filled tubes running through them. These tubes connect to a backpack on the suit that will chill and circulate the water. You need this because your sweat won't evaporate in a vacuum, and heat exhaustion would kill you.

Then comes your pressure suit, made of rubber and glue, much like something scuba divers wear. Your oxygen will come from your backpack. You will control the cooling system and oxygen supply by a remote control mounted on your chest.

▼ Armstrong's space suit preflight

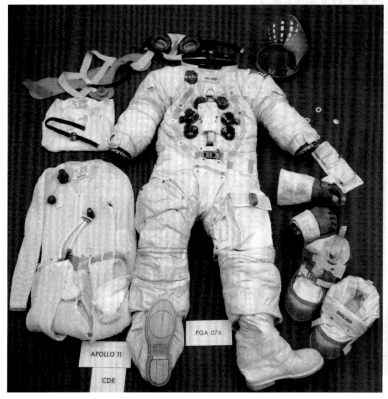

APOLLO 11

CDR

PGA 076

Now you zip your partner into a suit of armor, and your partner will do the same for you. It has 13 layers of special protective cloth, designed to prevent a puncture, which would kill you within a minute.

▲ Aldrin exits the *Eagle* and becomes the second person to stand on the moon. Armstrong, already on the surface, took this photograph.

You wear a skullcap connected to radio transmitters and receivers on your backpack. Your body sensors are connected to the radio system. Back at Mission Control in Houston, they will monitor your medical data.

You do allow yourself a little laugh during all the preparations. Much as the engineers tried to anticipate every possible problem and situation, they'd forgotten to put a handle on the outside of your Lunar Module. That means you have to remember not to lock the door hatch of the *Eagle* as you leave — or you'll be helpless on the outside, with no way to get back in.

Finally, you are ready. You exit and climb backward down the ladder. You are moving very slowly, but your heart is racing.

You are outside of the *Eagle!* You are about to step onto the moon!

Although there are no aliens visible, you are truly on an alien world. It is charcoal and gray. With dust that has never been shifted by wind or by water. With a sky that is completely black. With little atmosphere and no sounds.

Since the first humans existed on Earth and looked upward, the moon has been a mysterious light in the sky. And now, at the bottom of the ladder, you are only a very short distance from the moon's surface.

You jump down. Your left foot presses on the firm but grainy surface at exactly 10:56 p.m.

▲ Aldrin walks on the surface of the moon near a leg of the Lunar Module during the Apollo 11 EVA. The astronauts' bootprints are clearly visible.

Eastern Standard Time, July 21, 1969. Then both of your boots are planted on the surface of the moon.

You speak.

Your words have to cross nearly 250 000 mi. (400 000 km) of outer space. The radio waves garble it slightly. The millions upon millions on Earth who share this moment with you do not hear the word "a" in the phrase: "That's one small step for a man."

Instead, what reaches Earth are these words, destined to be as immortalized as the moon itself: "That's one small step for man, one giant leap for mankind."

Solve the Math Mystery

You are a Danish astronomer. It is 1676. You join the observatory of Uraniborg on the island of Hven, where Copernicus made his monumental observations generations before you. You observe more than 140 eclipses of Io, one of Jupiter's moons. You have a friend in Paris who has made the same observations. When you compare the times of the eclipses in both places, you are able to calculate the difference in longitude (the distance east and west) between Hven and Paris. This is what you had expected to be able to solve.

However, you have also noticed something strange. The time between the eclipses got shorter as Earth approached Jupiter, and longer as Earth moved away. Almost three centuries later, your solution to this puzzle will matter greatly to the epic journey to the moon.

Who are you, and what did you figure out?

Answer at end of the chapter.

STAGE TWO: A HOSTAGE SOVIET SPACECRAFT

There was a lot at stake the night that four U.S. spies took hostage a Russian spacecraft. It was 1959. Months before, Russia had managed impressive victories in their race to the moon against the United States. They'd succeeded in crashing *Luna 2* onto the moon. *Luna 3* brought the first ever photos of the far side of the moon. The Americans, on the other hand, had failed on their lunar missions.

This was at the height of the Cold War. On one side of the Pacific, Russia was the superpower that wanted to draw more countries into communism. On the other side was the superpower United States. The Americans wanted to spread democracy around the world.

Both sides were building up nuclear bombs, less as weaponry they wanted to use and more as a way to make sure the other side did not start a "hot" war that would take millions of lives, instead of the ongoing Cold War — "cold" because it was mostly threats and hostile behavior.

Winning the space race was seen as crucial to prestige. The two countries spied on each other, trying to get an upper hand in missile technology. The U.S. Central Intelligence Agency (CIA) was looking for ways to track Soviet lunar launches. But the exact specifications of the Soviet spacecraft were impossible to learn from the flares of rocket fires.

Then, Soviet pride came into play. Determined to show industrial superiority, the country put together a tour of their industrial achievements, which traveled

Soviet spacecraft
Luna 2

to several countries. This included a Soviet spacecraft, one of the *Lunas*.

To the astonishment of the CIA, this spacecraft was not a model, but the real thing. And it was heavily guarded.

Much the way a gang scouts out a bank before robbing it, the CIA looked for and finally found a weakness in Soviet security. The Soviets had a system for sending the spacecraft from city to city: moving it by truck to the railyard and then by train.

The CIA found a way to separate truck and driver. They moved the truck into an alley where they could lock it behind a gate. They had until dawn to learn as much as they could about the *Luna*.

First, they removed the roof of the truck, careful not to leave marks. It was of utmost importance that their efforts remain secret. If the Soviets found out, the diplomatic outrage could well lead to war. At the least, it would be extremely embarrassing for the United States if the rest of the world were to find out about their desperation to gain ground in the space race by stealing technology from the Russians.

With the roof of the truck removed, the real problems began. There were four CIA agents, but barely any room for them. They could not walk end to end. The *Luna* took up almost all of the room in the truck.

In stocking feet, they dropped down using rope ladders at the front and the back. In teams of two — one at each end — they used flashlights as they took apart what they could.

Then, they discovered that a plastic cap on the front end had a Soviet seal to prevent tampering. Their only choice was to radio back to headquarters to get a fake Soviet seal made as a replacement.

As early dawn approached, they scrambled to put everything back together, without leaving a trace of evidence. The last steps were to put the fake seal in place, carefully reinstall the roof and ensure the truck was driven back into place at the railway station.

With hundreds of photographs of the interior and exterior, the CIA had crucial information that allowed the Americans to learn what the Soviet technology could do — and what it couldn't do. They discovered they weren't as far behind as feared.

Just as important, they used the detailed information about the *Luna* to understand what was happening behind the flares of each new rocket launch.

It was information like this that gave U.S. President John F. Kennedy enough confidence to declare to the world that the Americans would put a man on the moon before the end of the 1960s.

In July of 1969, the Americans delivered on Kennedy's promise. Apollo 11 made its successful launch after the Russians had made a hurried and unwise attempt to beat them with a rocket that failed in a spectacular way only days before.

"We set sail on this new sea because there is a new knowledge to be gained, and new rights to be won, and they must be won and used for the progress of all people."

— *U.S. President Kennedy, speaking at Rice University in Texas in 1962*

STAGE THREE: THE MOON IS NOT A GIANT BALL

When is an egg shape actually a sphere?

One way to find out is to get in a spaceship and fly a couple of hundred thousand miles. Pull up beside the moon and glance over. From your new angle, you'll see that the moon is not a perfectly round ball, but is slightly egg-shaped.

Or, if you want to save a lot of time, grab an actual egg. Hold it at arm's length and point the small end toward you. What you'll see, of course, is a circle.

That's why the moon looks round to us. From Earth, we are seeing the small end of its true shape.

If you like knowing things to impress people or win bets, there's more.

Although we always see the exact same face of the moon, the truth is that it is rotating around its axis, in the same way that Earth rotates eastward around its own imaginary straw that pokes from the north pole through to the south pole. (To be totally accurate, this imaginary straw is not up and down for our planet, but tilted slightly. That's what causes our seasons. For half the year, one of the poles is tilted toward the sun, and for the other half of the year, it's tilted away.)

Why then, if the moon is rotating, do we always see the same face?

It's because the moon rotates so slowly, at only 10 mi. (16 km) per hour, compared to the roughly 1000 mi. (1600 km) per hour of the Earth's rotation.

▲ During its flight, NASA's *Galileo* spacecraft returned separate images of Earth and the moon, which were combined to create this photograph.

The moon has a 29-day orbit around our planet. That's also exactly how long it takes to make a single full rotation around its axis. This is not a coincidence. Over time, Earth's gravitational pull slowed down the rotation of the moon to match its orbital period. It turns out that this process is the same for many other planets with moons. As for Earth, that means that as the moon travels around us in a circle, the face of it never seems to change.

This also means that before space travel, humans had never seen the dark side of the moon. Although, again, to be accurate, the moon doesn't have a dark side. During part of the moon's orbit, it hangs between us and the sun, which means the lighted half faces away from us. On the other hand, when Earth hangs between the moon and the sun, we sometimes see full sunlight across the entire face of the moon. Other times, Earth makes a shadow across the moon. This is why we see different phases, like a half-moon or crescent moon.

By the way, because the moon's gravity causes our tides to slosh the waters of the oceans back and forth, the rotation of Earth has been gradually slowing. At one point, a long time ago, we had only 10 hours in a day instead of 24 hours.

Want even more moon facts to impress your friends? At any given time, there may be as many as 18 000 mini-moons that have the chance to be captured by Earth's gravity. Yup.

These are small asteroids caught in weird loops because of the competing gravities of the sun and the moon and the Earth. Until the sun finally tugs them away from us, some of them stay in orbit around us for a period of months, others for dozens of years. One large asteroid called Cruithne may stay caught in our gravity for another 5000 years, taking 770 years to make a single horseshoe-shaped orbit of our planet.

And you should know that in 1988, employees at the Lowell Observatory — a place in Arizona with telescopes to watch the night sky — ran a survey of the public. The results showed that 13 percent stated the moon was made of cheese. We can only hope these 13 percent were trying to be funny.

MathMysterySolved

Congratulations, Ole Christensen Rømer!

It takes you another eight years of observation and much trial and error, but you finally understand the principle behind what is happening and then come up with a mathematical formula that proves it.

Your hunch was that the delay between solar eclipses resulted from the different angles of Earth's position in relation to Jupiter. Your measures show that a delay of 22 minutes is the time needed for light to cross a distance equal to the diameter of Earth's orbit around the sun.

This reveals something staggering. Until your discovery, science assumed light moved at an infinite speed. But you have proven the opposite. It is not infinitely fast.

It will take more than 60 years for the scientific community to finally accept your conclusion and another 80 years or so for a final calculation of the speed of light: 186 000 mi. (300 000 km) per second. But the world now knows you were the first scientist to grasp a fundamental fact about the universe.

Without this knowledge, modern astronomy would not exist. Without modern astronomy, there would have been no first step on the moon.

+111:55:00

HOUR   MINUTE   SECOND

EPISODE NINE

MOONWALK

"This is the LM pilot. I'd like to take this opportunity to ask every person listening in, whoever and wherever they may be, to pause for a moment and contemplate the events of the past few hours, and to give thanks in his or her own way."

— *NASA transcript, Apollo 11 mission*

◄ Buzz Aldrin by the *Eagle*, preparing to deploy
the Early Apollo Scientific Experiments Package

STAGE ONE: THE KANGAROO HOP

▲ Buzz Aldrin, who piloted the first lunar landing, stands beside the United States flag.

The *Eagle* — ungainly as the design appears — looks magnificent. There is a gold coating on the bottom half. The upper half — designed to blast off and take you back to the *Columbia* — is bright silver for maximum visibility in outer space.

You look for Earth and see a swirl of clouds that reflects sunshine, and the blue of oceans. Its beauty takes your breath away.

Then there are two of you on the moon.

Only two hours are scheduled for this first moonwalk, and there is so much to do. But you go slowly. What could kill you now is a lack of discipline. If you overexert yourself, your body temperature will rise too high.

You take your first steps and discover something amazing. Your space suit, backpack and body weight add up to 353 lb. (160 kg). But in the low gravity of the moon, it's only 60 lb. (27 kg). When your legs are used to a far higher gravity, it feels like no work at all to walk on the moon.

And you discover it's easier to use a bouncing gait, like a kangaroo hop. You soon learn that you can't stop quickly.

Your gloves are so thick, it feels as if you have balloon hands. You reach down and scoop up as much dirt and rock as possible. You stuff it into a pocket of your space suit. If something goes wrong and you have to rush back into the *Eagle*, at least you'll have that sample of the moon to take home.

You now wait for the other astronaut in the *Eagle* to join you. All you hear is the hum of the pumps of your backpack as they circulate the fluid that keeps your body cool.

You are also amazed at what happens to the powder of the moon's surface. Because there is no air, each step causes an explosion of dust that sprays out in front of you, then falls in a perfect semicircle.

Everywhere you look, it's white and chalky gray. For billions of years, this has been a surface that has faced the inhospitable vacuum of outer space and the unrelenting full rays of the sun. You see thousands upon thousands of craters barely wider than a bathtub across. These are scars from the impact of tiny meteorites that are preserved forever in a windless, weather-less, airless environment.

What's really weird is the horizon. The moon is so much smaller than Earth that you can see the curvature. It's obvious to you that you are standing on a big ball.

These are things you notice as you gather dust and rock and soil samples and place them in sealed containers.

At the end of your time on the moon, you use a hand-powered pulley system to load the boxes into the upper half of the *Eagle*. You climb the ladder up past the lower half and squeeze inside the upper half. You seal the door and pressurize the cabin.

Your Extravehicular Activity (EVA) was 2 hours, 31 minutes and 40 seconds. To you, it felt like only a couple of heartbeats. It's over, and you wish you could have spent less time working and more time staring in awe at Earth and the stars and the craters around you.

Moon dust floats in the cabin. You wonder if there is a different kind of alien life form in it. Or something that will make you sick, something that will force you to spend the rest of your life on Earth in quarantine. You push that thought aside. It's a worry for the future. You have to get back to Earth first. Still, you plan to sleep with your helmet on to cut down on the dust — and to keep things quiet so you can finally rest.

▼ A close-up of an astronaut's boot and bootprint in the lunar soil

▲ Buzz Aldrin deploying the Early Apollo Scientific Experiments Package, which included the Passive Seismic Experiment and the Lunar Laser Ranging Retroreflector Array

You remove your EVA suit. Then you discard as much as possible — used filters and food packs, urine bags and diapers, suit, boots, backpack, cameras and visors. You need to lighten the load as much as possible for your launch back to the *Columbia*, where the third astronaut of

Apollo 11 has been waiting for you.

You reattach yourself to the *Eagle*'s life support system. You work through a long checklist to make sure everything is a go for the launch to take you back to the *Columbia*.

Then, as planned by Mission Control, you try to sleep before the countdown to liftoff. Although you have been awake for 22 hours and worked without pause, it isn't easy. Your mind races with the excitement and triumph of what you have done.

As you fall asleep, something incredible is happening 497 mi. (800 km) east of you. The Russians, still determined to come out ahead in the space race, have not given up after the explosion of their rocket ship a few weeks earlier.

Just days ahead of Apollo 11, the Russians sent out *Luna 15*, an unmanned rocket with a robotic probe. The Russians are planning to land it that very same night. They intend to scoop up lunar samples and return to Earth ahead of you. This will give them another win in the space race.

This would not matter to you. It's not what you are thinking most about. Because you have an unspoken worry, something few on Earth realize could end the Apollo 11 mission. Engineers consider the launch from the moon back to the *Columbia* the most dangerous part of the journey. Its success depends on one rocket engine and one switch to power the engine.

As you fall asleep, you have no idea that as you and the other astronaut undressed in the cramped space, one of you accidentally broke this crucial switch.

▲ A footpad of the Apollo 11 Lunar Module resting on the surface of the moon. The pole-like object sticking out is a lunar surface sensing probe.

Solve the Science Mystery

You are a British physicist so renowned that in 1904, you receive a Nobel Prize for discovering the gas argon. As important as this is to science, you also helped all of us with a question that nearly every child asks at one point or another.

While your answer might not have contributed to the epic journey to the moon, you surely would have satisfied the curiosity of the astronauts who traveled there. Because as children, they undoubtedly had that same question. After all, it was the sky that drew each of them upward, first as pilots, then as space travelers.

Who are you, and what question did you answer?

Answer at end of the chapter.

STAGE TWO: FIRST SPACE SURVIVORS

By any measure, space pioneers Belka and Strelka had rough lives in the Soviet Union. (Belka is Russian for "whitey," and Strelka means "little arrow.") With no parents to guide them, they lived on the streets, enduring cold weather and scavenging for food. But their ability to survive difficult conditions made them great candidates to become future heroes.

▲ Soviet space pioneers Belka and Strelka proved it was possible to survive in outer space.

Once taken off the streets, they endured a training schedule that proved how tough they were. Over the course of several weeks, they were put in smaller and smaller boxes until they became used to sitting motionless in cramped spaces for hours on end.

Neither complained about this treatment. Instead, they showed great patience and endurance.

Nor did they complain when they were dressed in custom-fitted space suits, then put in flight simulators to get accustomed to the forces that would be put on their bodies when their rocket launched.

When the day finally came, even after all this training, there were no guarantees they'd return alive. After all, the original Soviet canine team — Chaika and Lisichka — hadn't survived the rocket that exploded on the launch pad a month earlier. And during a much earlier launch, Laika had suffocated only a few hours into the flight.

Indeed, the television transmissions coming from their space capsule showed that neither Belka nor Strelka moved at all during their first three orbits of Earth.

The space doctors on Earth were worried as they observed what was happening up there in orbit. It was August of 1960, and nobody yet knew what the effects of zero gravity would be on hearts and lungs and muscles and brain tissue. Up there, was it possible for the complex body of a mammal to function without damage?

For three full orbits of Earth, Belka and Strelka remained in their trance. Neither moved, not even a little. What damage had they suffered? What might this mean for future astronauts? Was it even feasible to expect to survive outer space?

On the fourth orbit, Belka shuddered, then vomited. (Because Belka was not wearing a sealed helmet, there was no danger of inhaling the vomit and drowning.) This seemed to trigger Strelka out of a similar trance. Gradually, each became more alert.

They remained in space for 12 more orbits, proving it was possible to survive in outer space.

It was only one day in orbit, but as the first survivors of outer space, they were instant and worldwide celebrities upon their return to Earth. They were sent on tour in matching space suits — one red and one green — where onlookers adored their cheerful manner. They spent time on television. They met famous politicians in the Soviet Union and all across the world.

To the Russians, and indeed the rest of the world, they were heroes. Neither, however, seemed impressed that they had made history. What made them happy was that they were always given as much sausage as they could eat. After all, these two dogs had just convinced scientists that humans might be able to travel into space.

Indeed, less than a year later, Russian cosmonaut Yuri Gagarin became the first human in space, completing an orbital flight of 108 minutes in the *Vostok 1* spacecraft. It was never reported, however, if sausages were part of his reward after a successful return to Earth.

VALENTINA TERESHKOVA,
Cosmonaut

How do you become an astronaut without any pilot experience? It's simple, but not easy.

First, get good at parachuting.

Second, be willing to leap out into the air seconds before your space capsule crashes.

Third — and this is important — apply to be a cosmonaut, not an astronaut. In other words, be a citizen of the Soviet Union.

Because the American astronauts were first on the moon, the accomplishments of Russian cosmonauts often don't get the recognition they so deserve.

One of the reasons is Soviet secrecy. When the first woman in space almost became the first woman to die in space, that near disaster remained classified information for 40 years.

Valentina Tereshkova was that woman. Parachuting was her sport, and she'd jumped out of a plane 126 times before volunteering for the Soviet space program.

One of the differences in the early space program between the Russians and the Americans was that cosmonauts were required to parachute from their space capsules only seconds before ground impact.

Tereshkova had no experience as a pilot, but her parachuting skills got her accepted into the Soviet space program.

She was tested with gravity conditions that ranged from extreme gravity to weightlessness. She also had to prove she was capable of dealing with long periods of being alone.

On June 16, 1963, two years after Soviet Yuri Gagarin became the first man in space, Tereshkova became the first woman in space.

On her journey as the pilot of *Vostok 6* she orbited Earth 48 times for more than 70 hours. Her landing almost became a tragedy when an error in the navigation software caused her spacecraft to move away from Earth. When Tereshkova was alert enough to spot the error, Soviet scientists below developed a new landing program and she landed with only a bruise on her face.

As Tereshkova asked, "If women can be railroad workers in Russia, why can't they fly in space?"

As for that other space program, the one with astronauts, it wasn't until June 18, 1983 — nearly 20 years later — that the first American woman, Sally Ride, went to space.

◄ Valentina Tereshkova, the first woman in space

STAGE THREE: LUNAR LASER RANGING RETROREFLECTOR ARRAY

Maybe you've stood outside at night with a flashlight and shone the light upward, thinking how someday your beam would reach the other side of the universe. If so, sooner or later, you'd have another thought: not a chance. The flashlight beam isn't strong enough and the light scatters quickly.

In theory, however, it's not such a bad idea. Light, after all, does travel forward. You probably know that in a vacuum, it moves at an incredible speed — just short of 186 000 mi. (300 000 km) per second.

So when you glance at the sun, you are seeing it in the past, the way it was 8 minutes and 20 seconds earlier, when that light began to cross the 93 000 000 mi. (150 000 000 km) or so to reach Earth. If the sun died without warning, we wouldn't know for those 8-plus minutes.

The light from distant stars takes much longer to reach Earth. It's eerie to think that some of the stars you currently see at night may have already exploded and died, but the news, via the light traveling toward us, just hasn't reached Earth yet.

If you could convert your flashlight into a

▲ Apollo 11, 14 and 15 astronauts placed Lunar Laser Ranging Retroreflector Arrays on the surface of the moon.

laser, then your concept about shining your light across the universe would take a giant step toward reality.

This, in fact, was what scientists had in mind when they requested that Armstrong and Aldrin place something called a Lunar Laser Ranging Retroreflector Array on the moon — which would be, well, a panel with a bunch of mirrors, described in fancy engineering terms. One hundred mirrors, to be exact, pointing at Earth.

With about an hour to go in their final moonwalk, that's exactly what Armstrong and Aldrin did. The panel with mirrors is still there, surrounded by their footprints, which will remain for millions of years. (On the moon, there is no weather and almost no wind to destroy their boot marks in the dust.)

Because the lunar mirrors don't need power, it's the only Apollo science experiment that is still running all these years later.

The mirrors are corner cube reflectors. That means any laser beam that hits the mirror shoots straight back to where it came from.

The word "laser" stands for — take a deep breath before you say it — Light Amplification by Stimulated Emission of Radiation. Just think of a laser as really concentrated light.

On Earth, astronomers and scientists shoot laser pulses out of a telescope at this mirror on the moon, and wait for a return flash of light.

By measuring the rate of the flash, we know now that, sadly, the moon is a thief making the slowest getaway in history. The moon's pull of gravity steals some of Earth's rotational energy, which is why our days get fractionally longer with each passing century and why once, a very long time ago, Earth had 10-hour days. The moon uses this stolen energy to boost itself 1½ in. (3.8 cm) higher in orbit every year.

That might not sound like much, but over a million years, that adds up to more than 20 mi. (32 km). And a million years isn't much time to a solar system. There was a time when the moon was only 14 000 mi. (22 500 km) from Earth, compared to its average distance away from us today of 238 856 mi. (384 402 km).

Good thing, then, that we made sure to fly to the moon in 1969. We saved some fuel because the journey was a little shorter then than it is now.

▲ Scientists plan to do lunar laser ranging at the Goddard Geophysical and Astronomical Observatory north of Glenn Dale, MD.

ScienceMysterySolved

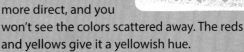

Congratulations, John William Strutt!

You are the third Baron Rayleigh, and you discovered and measured the effect named after you, "Rayleigh scattering." That's the short answer to one of our most important childhood questions: Why is the sky blue?

The longer answer is that light from the sun bounces off molecules of gas and other particles in the atmosphere. The amount of bounce is dependent on the wavelength of the light. The shorter the wavelength, the more the bounce, or scatter. (You might remember that when white light goes through a prism, it breaks down into the various spectrums or colors.) The blue light in sunlight has a shorter wavelength than red light, for example. This means that blues and greens get scattered the most in all directions. In combination, blues and greens give the sky its pale blue light. If you glance at the sun, however, the light is more direct, and you won't see the colors scattered away. The reds and yellows give it a yellowish hue.

As for reds at dawn or sunset? Light near the horizon passes through a bigger part of the atmosphere, and the shorter wavelengths of blue and green are removed by the extra bouncing they take to reach your eyes, leaving mainly reds.

The astronauts most certainly discovered this in a dramatic way once they were in outer space. With no atmosphere to produce Rayleigh scattering, the sun is simply white and space is simply black, as proven in color film photographs from the moonwalk.

+124:03:00

HOUR   MINUTE   SECOND

EPISODE TEN

STRANDED FOREVER?

"We have four pressure talkbacks indicating red. We still have the circuit breakers out as of right now ... Is it normal to have these four red flags?"

— *NASA transcript, Apollo 11 mission*

◄ The *Eagle*, the moon and Earth beyond, just before rendezvous with the *Columbia*

STAGE ONE: SAVED BY A PEN

▲ The Lunar Module had two stages. Its lower, or descent, stage had the gear, engines and fuel needed for the landing. That stage also served as a launching pad when the upper, or ascent, stage, where the two astronauts lived while on the moon, blasted off to meet the *Columbia*.

however, it is not tasty. After all, it was freeze-dried.

Still, you need energy to be as alert and focused as possible for lunar liftoff.

Making it to the moon and back depends on a long chain of events, and all have to be successful. As you were trying to fall asleep, it occurred to you that this next event is the link that Mission Control believes has the highest possibility of breaking that chain.

Almost every other aspect of the Apollo 11 journey was designed so that if one part broke down, another could replace it. In engineering design, this is called "redundancy." In some cases, engineers designed redundancies for the original redundancy. Obviously, on this journey, there is no way to find a repair shop.

For the lunar ascent, however, there was no option to add a second rocket engine in case the first one failed. It would have added too much weight to the upper half of the *Eagle*.

In short, if this one engine fails, you are stuck on the moon. There is

You did not have a good sleep. The *Eagle* dropped in temperature and grew too cold to be comfortable. But opening the shades to warm your tiny living space would make it too warm and flood the *Eagle* with sunlight that would make it impossible to sleep.

You are tired. You force yourself to eat a freeze-dried breakfast. Bacon, peaches and cookies. It sounds good, in theory. In practice,

no other way that you can leave.

What you have in your favor is that — because there is no redundancy — the *Eagle*'s single remaining rocket engine may well be the best-designed and best-tested engine in human existence.

The only moving part is a ball valve that will allow two components of fuel to meet and mix in the rocket chamber. These fuels are called "hypergolic." That means they ignite on contact with each other. Hypergolic fuel eliminates the need for any additional part that can fail.

So. One ball valve. One rocket chamber. One control switch that is either on or off. Tested again and again and again at the design stage to be fail-proof.

Still, this is rocketry. Involving explosions. Failures are a possibility. And it depends on that one switch, marked Proceed.

The rocket is so powerful and the *Eagle*'s top half so light that, with the moon's gravity at one-sixth of Earth's, the self-igniting fuel will thrust you from 0 to 3000 mi. (4830 km) per hour in two minutes.

Except there is a limited time window for launch: too soon or too late, and you miss the orbit of the *Columbia* above you. You need perfect timing to catch that ride home.

Once you punch the button for ignition, the explosive bolts holding the upper half of the *Eagle* to the lower half have to explode and cut all connections. Instantly.

In theory, it works. But this final phase was impossible to test on Earth because the conditions you face here on the moon are so, well, unearthly.

You go through your checklist. You turn off the radar system that will help you meet the *Columbia* as it orbits. The engineers don't want the computer overload you faced on the way down to the moon.

▼ NASA sketches illustrate the steps taken when the astronauts left the moon.

Ascent Stage Launch

Rendezvous and Docking

LM Jettison

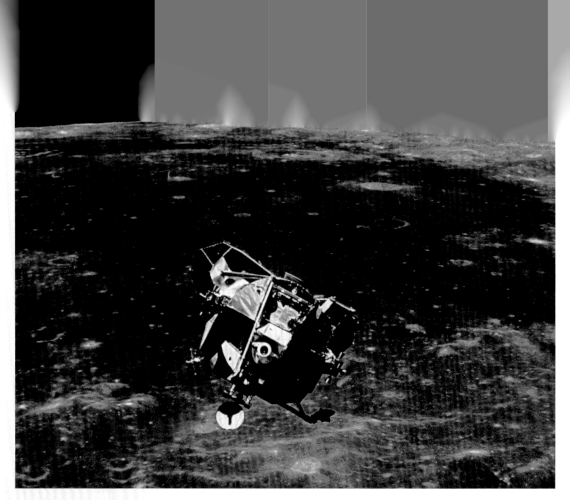

▲ The Lunar Module, the *Eagle*, had an engine to lift it off the moon and send it toward the orbiting Command and Service Module, the *Columbia*. The *Eagle* appears here above the moon, with Earth beyond, just before rendezvous.

Near the end of your checklist, you test the altitude thrusters. All is good.

Then you fire a small charge to open the engine's helium tanks.

You stare at the gauges in disbelief. They show no pressure in the tanks.

No pressure.

Either the tanks didn't open, or the gauges are wrong.

Either way, this is not a problem you can fix. Either way, you have to continue the countdown and hope the problem is a stuck gauge.

Now you arm the explosive bolts that will snap you apart from the lower half of the *Eagle*. Then, you reach for a switch to arm the rocket.

That's when you see a small black object in the corner, on the floor.

Again, you feel disbelief. It's the end of a circuit breaker. It must have broken off while you were removing your space suit.

You look up at the rows and rows of electrical circuit breakers.

This is incredible. The only one that is broken is the one needed to arm the engine to ignite — the single engine that your return to Earth depends upon.

Broken.

This is your situation. Time is passing and you are about to lose the window of opportunity to meet the *Columbia*.

There may or may not be helium in the tanks.

And the single most crucial switch for your journey home will not work because the circuit breaker for it has broken off.

You are about to be marooned. Unlike the sailors of the past, however, you have no hope that any ship can give rescue.

In a flash of inspiration, you find a felt-tip pen. You jam it into the space that you see in the broken switch.

It works.

It works!

The bolts explode in the same instant that the rocket fires. There is a powerful upward thrust. The upper half of the *Eagle* begins to rise.

Liftoff!

Behind you, 497 mi. (800 km) away, is the wreckage from the one that didn't make it, a demonstration of what can so easily go wrong. But you are unaware that *Luna 15* — the Soviet attempt to be the first to bring back lunar samples — had crashed into a mountain on the moon and ceased to send out any more transmissions.

And you?

You are alive and headed back to the *Columbia*. You averted disaster and saved the mission with something as simple as a Sharpie.

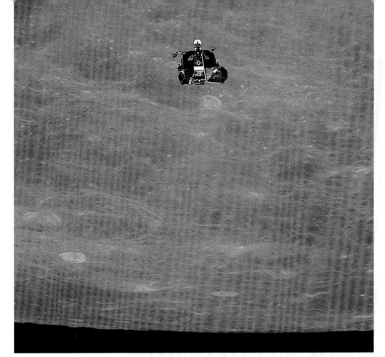

▲ The Apollo 11 Lunar Module ascent stage

SOLVE THE TECHNOLOGY MYSTERY

You are an Italian scientist. It is 1799. One of your peers is an Italian physicist named Luigi Galvani, who discovered something called "animal electricity." Galvani used two thin strips of two different kinds of metal to connect to the nerves of a frog's legs in a linked series, and this produced electricity. His experiment appears to confirm the theory of the time — that electricity is generated solely by living beings.

You, however, wonder if the truth might be the opposite. Instead of the frog's legs producing electricity, perhaps the legs are simply allowing electricity to pass through — conducting electricity.

You have a hunch about the different metals that Galvani uses in the experiments. And you wonder if you can prove your theory to the world. You are unaware of how much your insight — and the proof of it — will matter to the epic journey to the moon.

Who are you, and what did you prove?

Answer at end of the chapter.

Stage Two: Apollo 13's Great Escape

At first, the astronauts of Apollo 13 (two missions after Apollo 11) thought the Command Module had been hit by a meteoroid. They had almost reached the moon and, until then, it had been a routine mission for James Lovell, John Swigert and Fred Haise.

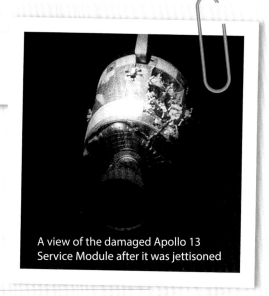

A view of the damaged Apollo 13 Service Module after it was jettisoned

Yes. Routine. Apollo 11 had been heralded as the most amazing technological feat in human history. Apollo 12 put two more astronauts on the moon.

In April of 1970, Apollo 13's Command and Service Module, named *Odyssey*, and the Lunar Module, named *Aquarius*, had already reached the spaceflight record for farthest distance from Earth. Although it was a televised trip, people around the world did not stop what they were doing to see yet another moon landing.

That changed at Ground Elapsed Time 55:54:53 with a bang.

The crew did not know if it was space debris or an accidental explosion. They had no idea that an entire panel had been blown off the Service Module part of the *Odyssey*.

Immediately, the gauge for oxygen tank two showed zero. Then two of the three fuel cells failed. Looking outside the window of the *Odyssey*, it was obvious that gas was escaping. About two hours later, the remaining oxygen was gone. All of the *Odyssey*'s electrical power was generated by combining oxygen and hydrogen. The last fuel cell shut down, leaving only a reserve battery crucial for reentry into Earth's atmosphere. The crew had no choice but to shut down the *Odyssey* completely.

It was still attached to the *Aquarius*, so all three astronauts transferred themselves through the tunnel into the cramped space of the *Aquarius*. They sealed the hatch between the two vessels. The *Aquarius* had essentially become a lifeboat.

But this lifeboat needed to take them 200 000 mi. (322 000 km) back to Earth. And because it was a Lunar Module, it only had enough food and water for two people to last a day and a half. Now there were three, and the trip to Earth would take four days.

This was the least of the problems. Yes, there was enough oxygen. But when humans breathe, they create carbon dioxide (CO_2). There wasn't enough power for the filters that removed CO_2 from the air. Too soon, the astronauts would suffocate.

Engineers at Houston found a way to get past that problem by adapting lithium hydroxide canisters from the *Odyssey*.

Then the astronauts faced their next obstacle.

The *Odyssey* was completely powered down. The *Aquarius* was down to the lowest power setting possible to preserve battery life.

By then, the failures of Apollo 13 were drawing as much attention around the world as had the successes of Apollo 11.

Would these three astronauts be stranded to forever circle the solar system in an icy tomb, their bodies perfectly preserved?

Mission Control in Houston had to invent an entirely new start-up system, then trust it would work in practice the way they calculated it would work in theory.

The audience across the world was mesmerized by this real-life drama over the hours it took for this solution to unfold.

Yes! It worked! The *Odyssey* was operational again, with just enough battery power for the control it needed during reentry.

But now the CM and LM had to be separated. The *Aquarius*, after all, had not been designed as a lifeboat. It was built to take astronauts from the *Odyssey* down to the moon. The lower part would stay on the moon. The upper part would take them back to the *Odyssey*, then be discarded.

Now, both spacecraft were still attached, and rapidly approaching Earth. With no power to pop them apart.

A team of engineers in Canada were given the problem to solve. They decided that using the remaining air to pressurize the tunnel between the *Odyssey* and the *Aquarius* would be enough to pop them apart. But the pressure had to be perfect. Not enough, no pop. Too much, the hatch would be damaged and the astronauts would burn into carbon dust.

The engineers did their calculations again and again. There was no room for the tiniest mistake. They sent the results to Mission Control, who radioed the numbers to the astronauts.

For hours, a worldwide audience tracked the crew on its way home. Each new problem and solution took them on a roller coaster of emotions.

The astronauts moved back into the *Odyssey* and sealed the tunnel hatch. If it didn't disconnect from the *Aquarius*, all the other problems they had solved would be meaningless. The world below would watch their deaths by television.

Yes! Again! The solution worked.

The *Odyssey* detached, barely in time for reentry. The now-empty *Aquarius* trailed behind into Earth's atmosphere and burned as quickly as any meteor.

As for the *Odyssey*, the world cheered as wildly at the sight of it hanging from parachutes above the ocean, ready to splash down safely, as it had when Neil Armstrong took those first steps.

Houston Mission Control Center

"Houston, we have a problem." You may have heard this phrase before. People often use it when trouble happens. It refers to the Houston Mission Control Center, where dozens of engineers and controllers monitored Apollo missions.

The phrase, while not quite word-for-word accurate, is familiar to many from the movie *Apollo 13*. Here's the real conversation:

> [Astronaut] Swigert: "Okay, Houston, we've had a problem here."
>
> [Houston MCC] Lousma: "This is Houston. Say again, please."
>
> [Astronaut] Lovell: "Uh, Houston, we've had a problem."

◀ Apollo 13 astronauts Fred W. Haise Jr., James A. Lovell Jr. and John L. Swigert Jr.

STAGE THREE: THE PRESIDENTIAL SPEECH THE WORLD DID NOT HEAR

Everyone at NASA, including the astronauts, knew the great moment of truth for Apollo 11 would be the *Eagle*'s launch back to the *Columbia*, where Michael Collins was waiting in lunar orbit for Neil Armstrong and Buzz Aldrin to return.

If there was any kind of mishap and the *Eagle* could not launch, Armstrong and Aldrin would be stranded there. Publicly, the phrase used was "close down communication." But the horrible reality was that — with hundreds of millions of people across the world watching the mission on television — Mission Control would have no choice but to leave them there to starve to death or commit suicide.

That's why Apollo 8 astronaut Frank Borman, who was also the go-between for NASA with the White House, had made a phone call a few days before the Apollo 11 mission. He spoke with President Nixon's speechwriter and suggested that the president have a speech ready in case the *Eagle* was unable to launch.

This speech, called "In Event of Moon Disaster," was kept from the public until 1999.

Had Aldrin not been able to jam a felt-tip pen into the broken switch and brilliantly save the mission, this is what the world would have heard from President Nixon as both astronauts were abandoned to their doom in the absolute cold of outer space:

▲ The Apollo 11 crew portrait. Left to right: Neil A. Armstrong, commander; Michael Collins, Command Module pilot; Edwin E. "Buzz" Aldrin, Lunar Module pilot.

In Event of Moon Disaster

Fate has ordained that the men who went to the moon to explore in peace will stay on the moon to rest in peace.

These brave men, Neil Armstrong and Edwin Aldrin, know that there is no hope for their recovery. But they also know that there is hope for mankind in their sacrifice.

These two men are laying down their lives in mankind's most noble goal: the search for truth and understanding.

They will be mourned by their families and friends; they will be mourned by their nation; they will be mourned by the people of the world; they will be mourned by a Mother Earth that dared send two of her sons into the unknown.

In their exploration, they stirred the people of the world to feel as one; in their sacrifice, they bind more tightly the brotherhood of man.

In ancient days, men looked at stars and saw their heroes in the constellations. In modern times, we do much the same, but our heroes are epic men of flesh and blood.

Others will follow, and surely find their way home. Man's search will not be denied. But these men were the first, and they will remain the foremost in our hearts.

For every human being who looks up at the moon in the nights to come will know that there is some corner of another world that is forever mankind.

TECHNOLOGY MYSTERY SOLVED

Congratulations, Alessandro Volta!

You decide to try Galvani's experiment with something other than frog legs. You use that same series of linked metals to connect with paper soaked in salt water. You discovered that, yes, there was the same flow of electricity. The paper in brine, like the frog's legs, allows electricity to flow.

If, as you suspected, the electricity was not being produced by a living animal, you were forced to conclude that somehow it was the combination of the different metals. You proved electricity could be generated chemically and not solely by living beings.

With more experiments, you learned that combining zinc and copper was the most effective way to generate that flow. As a result, you invented an early form of battery, named after you — the voltaic pile. (And of course, the "volt" in "volts of electricity.")

The epic journey to the moon depended heavily on batteries to store electricity. Without your discovery, Alessandro Volta, there wouldn't have been reserve power when needed during all parts of the journey to the moon, including the crucial lunar launch back to the *Columbia*.

+127:55:00

HOUR   MINUTE   SECOND

EPISODE ELEVEN

THE BIG BURN

"The responsibility for this flight lies first with history and the giants of science who have preceded this effort."

— *NASA transcript, Apollo 11 mission*

◄ On July 24, 1969, after splashdown, three Apollo 11 crew members await a helicopter ride to the recovery ship USS *Hornet*.

STAGE ONE: HIT, MISS, HIT

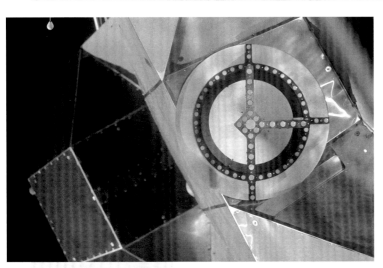

▲ A very close view of the docking target on the *Eagle* photographed from the *Columbia* during their reconnection in lunar orbit

You have made it to moon orbit, but at the wrong level. You are zipping around the moon at more than 1 mi. (1.6 km) per second, some 3600 mi. (5800 km) per hour. But you need to find the *Columbia*, which is still above you. And you need to slow down. Drastically.

You burn more fuel. Forty-five more seconds. You and the *Eagle* rise a dozen or so miles. You also slow your speed to a mere 131 ft. (40 m) per second, maybe 90 mi. (145 km) per hour.

You let out a breath of relief when you spot the *Columbia*'s lights. The two spacecraft are mere specks in a limitless universe. But how wonderful that the speck with the lights is home.

Not that you are through the door yet. Powered by two very small burns of the *Eagle*'s rocket engine, you line up with the *Columbia*. You are synced in orbit, performing a beautiful dance around the moon.

It takes two full orbits to line up the head of the *Eagle* to the head of the *Columbia*. Now it's a reverse of the disconnection. You are pointing your drogue — the circular plate with a hole in it — at the *Columbia*'s probe.

As they connect, you hit a switch that fires a little gas bottle. This, in turn, fires a plunger to pull both spacecraft — *Columbia* and *Eagle* — together. At the same time, 12 capture latches pop forward mechanically to secure one spacecraft to the other.

Yet, just as you fire it, the drogue sheers sideways. It's a miss.

Another miss. On autopilot, the navigation system gyroscopes have gone into a lock.

Each attempt throws the *Eagle* and then the *Columbia* sideways. It's a clumsy wrestling match.

You need to connect! The *Columbia* is your ship home.

You switch from autopilot to abort guidance system — AGS. Once again, you need your human

piloting skills to do what the computer can't do.

Then *bang!* This is the sweet sound of 12 big latches slamming into place. It's a lock.

You can open the hatch between the *Eagle* and the *Columbia*. You reunite with the third astronaut and it leads to hugs and giggles. You did it!

Now, there's work ahead of you. You transfer the vacuum-packed boxes of lunar rocks to the *Columbia* from the *Eagle*.

You move as much unneeded gear as you can from the *Columbia* back into the *Eagle* to lighten your load for the trip back to Earth.

You seal the hatch. You pop the latches and release the *Eagle*. You watch it drift away with a mixture of relief and sadness. In time, it will lose orbit and crash into the moon.

In constant communication with Houston, you turn your attention to escaping the moon: trans-Earth injection. The *Columbia* is still attached to its Service Module. You fire up the SM's rocket engine and burn 9920 lb. (4500 kg) of gas in 2 minutes, 30 seconds. You boost the *Columbia*'s speed to 5300 mi. (8530 km) per hour, and you slingshot around the dark side of the moon on a path to take you home.

KATHERINE JOHNSON,
Human Computer

In an era when computers that can solve an almost infinite number of problems fit inside something as small as a wristwatch, it's sometimes difficult to imagine that NASA depended on human brains to crunch the numbers for complex mathematical problems.

For these tasks, NASA drew upon the work of a group of African American women whose crucial role in space travel remained almost unknown until it was celebrated in the book and movie *Hidden Figures*.

One of those women, Katherine Johnson, was a numbers genius. She would simply ask when and where on Earth NASA wanted a capsule to land after orbiting the planet, and then she would work out the geometry backward from that location. It was Johnson who calculated the arcs and curves of Alan Shepard's historic first American flight into space in 1961. And in 1962, when John Glenn was preparing to become the first American to orbit Earth, he didn't trust the equations programmed by computers. During the preflight checklist, he asked for Johnson to verify the computer numbers, saying, "If she says they're good, then I'm ready to go."

Johnson feels her greatest contribution to space exploration was her calculations for the Apollo 11 mission, when she helped sync the orbit of the Lunar Module to allow it to reconnect with the Command and Service Module as it circled the moon.

For years, every time a man walked on the moon, Johnson and the other "female computers" played a huge but uncelebrated role in making that event possible.

Then in 2015, at age 97, Johnson received the Presidential Medal of Freedom. And the place at Langley where she used to work? It's now called the Katherine G. Johnson Computational Research Facility.

The rest of the three-day journey to Earth should be uneventful. But midway, Mission Control radio picks up mysterious sounds. Mission Control is highly disturbed. They hear whistling sounds and bells. They call in. "You sure you don't have anybody else in there with you?"

You have no answer for Mission Control. The mystery grows. Some speculate that the noise came from aliens. How, they wonder, did those sounds break into the radio transmissions from outer space?

You, however, have more important matters on your mind. You are about to face your final deadly challenge to a safe return to Earth: the same factor that protects the planet from most meteors.

Anything that hits the atmosphere at speed burns from the friction against air. It's a spectacular burn, generating the shooting stars that appear and vanish so quickly in the night skies.

You don't want to be that shooting star. The only way to avoid that, however, is to hit the atmosphere at exactly the correct angle. Too steep, and fire destroys you and the *Columbia*. Too shallow, you and the *Columbia* bounce away, with not enough fuel to turn around and try again.

This angle is precisely six degrees.

Then comes the news of an added difficulty — not with the *Columbia* but with equipment on Earth. One of the antennae tracking you by radio is stuck. A bearing has failed at a crucial rotation point of the machinery. If it isn't fixed, you may lose communication in the last segment of your journey. There is no time for regular repairs. But it's almost impossible to access — unless you are the station director's 10-year-old son. He reaches into the small space and packs the bearing with grease, the fix works, and you are guaranteed radio communication all the way in.

Just before reaching the atmosphere, you separate and

▼ The Apollo 16 Command Module splashed down in the Pacific Ocean on April 27, 1972, after an 11-day moon mission, the sixth crewed exploration of the moon.

eject the Service Module from the Command Module. You have no power, but gravity will pull you down at a terrifying speed — which means you have to depend on parachutes packed weeks earlier, folded parachutes that traveled to the moon and back.

The last words from Houston before reentry? "Have a good trip … and remember to come in BEF."

That's right. Blunt End Forward. The *Columbia* is now moving at 25 000 mi. (40 235 km) per hour. (A rifle bullet travels at 2000 mi. [3220 km] per hour.) Blunt End Forward means facing backward, with the heat shield forward.

The heat shield is designed to burn and take away heat with it. This means you become a comet, with orange-yellow in the center of the tail and edges of lavender and blue.

The shield heats up to 5000°F (2760°C), almost enough to melt a diamond. For four minutes, the *Columbia* is literally on fire, and you see the flames streaming around you.

You brace for the giant jolt of opening parachutes. Acres of cloth to slow your descent. The jolt comes. You grin. You are about to land in the swells of the Pacific Ocean. But helicopters are on standby.

You are home! Safe!

From here, your future depends on a small colony of white mice that have been bred specifically for your return to Earth. And you won't know your fate for weeks.

▲ The Apollo 11 spacecraft Command Module being lowered to the deck of the USS *Hornet*. The flotation ring Navy divers attached to the capsule has been removed.

Solve the Science Mystery

You are a botanist. You live in Scotland. It is the year 1827. There are another 142 years remaining in the epic journey to the moon.

As a scientist who studies plants, you have observed the strange movement of pollen suspended in water in a glass jar. (Pollen are tiny, tiny grains of seeds released by flowers.) You have noticed that no matter how long you wait for the water to settle, the pollen keep bouncing around as if they are alive.

Something must be causing this. But what?

And how will your answer stop the future Apollo 11 astronauts from dying in a fire as hot as the sun on their return into the bubble of air around Earth?

Who are you, and what did you discover?

Answer at end of the chapter.

Looking back, sometimes it's difficult to understand how much was at stake in the space race between the United States and Russia. Worldwide prestige mattered, of course. But each side wanted to prove to the other that it had superior technology. Each side wanted the other to be afraid of starting a war it would lose to the other side's superior technology.

We've learned that the Americans were worried enough to use spies to try to stay ahead of the Russians.

Here's a thought, then. What if the U.S. government was so desperate that somebody high up decided to fake the moon landing?

All you'd need is a good studio and willing actors. Then you could feed the footage to an unsuspecting world. A lot of things point to this.

Ever seen that photograph of a footprint on the moon? You'd need moisture in the sand for it to hold like that. There is no moisture on the moon.

There's famous footage of the U.S. flag on the moon, and it shows the flag with ripples. You can't have ripples without wind. There is no wind on the moon.

The temperature on the moon is 284°F (140°C). Camera film would melt in that temperature. And notice the high quality of those photographs? There must have been professional photographers involved, not astronauts.

There's no blast crater in the photographs. Weird, then, that the Lunar Module, with a weight of 34 000 lb. (15 400 kg), sits on top of sand, while right beside it are astronaut footprints.

In the footage shown on television, when the Lunar Module takes off, there are no flames from the rocket. And ever notice there are no stars in the background sky in the photographs?

One other thing. If Armstrong was the first human on the moon, why is there footage of him stepping down from the *Eagle*? Someone else must have been there to film him — as he faked the first step on the moon.

▲ Astronaut Neil A. Armstrong, Apollo 11 commander, as televised seconds before that first step on the moon. Not everyone watching at home believed the moment was real.

If all of this leads you to start doubting whether the moon landing happened on July 20, 1969, you are not alone.

What might be fun, however, is trying something out for yourself to see what is true or fake.

Start with a tray filled with talcum powder (very fine powder). Use something to make an impression in it. You'll discover that even though the powder is extremely dry, it holds a crisp impression. Lunar sand has never faced erosion by wind or water. The grains have sharp edges and form a fine talcum that, yes, holds impressions of a footprint. Your own experiment will confirm that the powder does not need moisture to hold a footprint.

You can't have ripples without wind. There is no wind on the moon. There are no stars in the background sky.

A rippling flag? The top of the flag had a horizontal bar in it to keep the flag from drooping. The soil was so hard that Armstrong and Aldrin had to bang the flagpole repeatedly to jam it in the ground. This left both the pole and the horizontal bar of the flag rocking back and forth during the time they filmed it. And, in a vacuum, vibrations continue a lot longer.

Why wouldn't the camera film melt? Nobody took out bare film and left it on the hot surface of the moon. The film was always protected in high-tech cameras or canisters. And the Apollo missions landed either at dawn or dusk, when the temperatures were much lower.

High-quality photographs? Absolutely! NASA published only the best.

No blast crater? The Lunar Module touched down on solid rock that was covered in only a light layer of moon dust — enough dust for footprints, but not enough for the module to sink. And in only one-sixth of Earth's gravity, the rocket thrusters didn't have to use the kind of power needed elsewhere. There simply wasn't enough thrust to scorch solid rock.

No flames from the thruster? The rocket fuel — hydrazine and dinitrogen tetroxide — does not burn with a visible flame. Not on Earth. Not on the moon. Never.

No stars in the background? Not with the sun's light so bright that the film exposure was too short to capture the much dimmer light of stars.

As for the mystery of who filmed Armstrong's first step onto the moon? The camera was waiting on a pallet on the side of the *Eagle* in the Modularized Equipment Stowage Assembly. From inside the *Eagle*, all that Aldrin had to do was yank on a cord and flip a switch to activate the television camera.

Since the moon landing, geologists and scientists from across the world all are in agreement that the Apollo rocks came from the moon. If anybody could find the slightest reason to prove the rocks are fake, you can be certain it would have happened.

Since the moon landing, there have been decades of laser pulses shot from telescopes at the mirrors on the moon. It's impossible for this to happen unless humans were on the moon to place the mirrors on the surface.

In short, it's fun to talk about a conspiracy that faked the moon landing. But that's all it could ever be. Just talk.

If you wear glasses, you'll need to thank NASA.

To begin with, it might never have occurred to you why they are called glasses. The answer, obvious as it sounds, is that eyeglasses were once manufactured with glass. Eyeglasses then were heavy and dangerous; shattered eyeglasses too often sent shards of glass into vulnerable eyeballs. It was so dangerous, in fact, that new laws eventually forced all manufacturers of prescription lenses and sunglasses to switch to plastic.

So, based on the percentage of people who wear glasses, there's a good chance that you are using NASA technology to read this book.

The downside to plastic lenses is that they scratch far too easily. A NASA researcher was working on a water purification system and found a new way to coat filters with a thin plastic film that was amazingly tough. NASA then used this technique to develop a scratch-resistant coating for the space helmet visors. Today, because of that technique, nearly all eyeglasses sold are coated with the same protective layer, and plastic lenses last 10 times longer than before.

If you wear running shoes, you'll need to thank NASA.

To produce helmets for outer space, NASA invented a process known as "blow rubber molding." After engineer Frank Rudy left NASA, he thought this system might work well as a shock absorber, because it formed a pad with interconnected air cells. He wondered if a company called Nike might like to use it to cushion heels against the impact of hitting the ground. Nike did. And called it Nike Air.

Do you work in construction? Or suck up the dust in your home with a cordless vacuum? You'll need to thank NASA.

One of an astronaut's jobs on the moon was to drill into rock to get samples. There aren't many places with electrical outlets to plug in a drill on the moon — okay, none. NASA went to a company named Black & Decker and asked for a special lightweight drill that could be powered by batteries. It not only turned out to be a huge success on the moon, but it spawned an entire industry of cordless tools used every day in the medical, home consumer and construction industries.

◄ Buzz Aldrin's Omega Speedmaster watch was attached to a long strip of Velcro that could wrap around his wrist or attach to the sleeve of his space suit during a spacewalk.

And thanks, too, for this small sample out of your thousands of patented inventions necessary for space travel:

COMPUTER MICROCHIPS: Circuits used in the Apollo Guidance Computer on board the Command Modules are the basis for modern computer chips.

FREEZE-DRIED FOOD: Well, maybe not such a big thank you there. Have you ever tasted freeze-dried food?

JOYSTICKS: First used by astronauts on the Apollo Lunar Rover for lunar transportation during later Apollo missions, joysticks were adapted for computer games.

SATELLITE TELEVISION: The technology used to fix errors in spacecraft signals is now used to reduce scrambled pictures by capturing television signals via satellite (which more than makes up for the freeze-dried food).

INSULATION: The reflective material invented to protect spacecraft from radiation is now used to insulate homes.

MODERN SMOKE DETECTORS: NASA invented the first smoke detector with sensitivity alarms.

CARBON WATER FILTERS: Techniques NASA invented to kill bacteria in the water supplies used in outer space are now used in water filters.

Thanks a lot, NASA!

► Technology from astronauts' space suits was used to make firefighters' clothing lightweight, fire-resistant and heat-protective.

◄ Cordless tools were first developed for use on space missions.

ScienceMysterySolved

Congratulations, Robert Brown!

You first had a weird thought, and then you were able to prove it. You realized that pollen suspended in water get bounced around by something surrounding them that doesn't stop vibrating — molecules. Your theory became known as "Brownian motion" and is considered one of the most important observations of your century.

Why did this matter to our future astronauts?

At sea level, the molecules of oxygen and nitrogen in the air are packed very densely. At the outer atmosphere, however, there are only about a dozen molecules of atmosphere gas scattered in a space the size of a cube big enough to swallow New York City. Even so, given the speed of reentry, if the space capsule enters at an angle that is too steep, hitting those molecules will cause enough friction to explode it.

But if the capsule approaches at an angle that is too shallow, it will skip off Earth's atmosphere and bounce back into space, sending the astronauts on a cold journey that will never end as it drifts through the universe.

Congratulations, Robert Brown. Understanding the existence of molecules and how they work was a huge step in the amazing and epic journey to the moon.

EPILOGUE: JOURNEY'S END

"You sure you don't have anybody else in there with you?"

— *NASA transcript, Apollo 11 mission*

Somewhere in the Pacific Ocean in the dark, you are strapped in and hanging from the ceiling of the *Columbia*. The waves are taller than you are. Those waves slapped and engulfed your parachutes, then flipped the *Columbia* upside down.

Previous astronauts learned the hard way that seasickness is a real danger. You don't want to vomit now. You've taken seasickness pills and all you need to do is wait for rescue.

Four Sea King helicopters arrive with Navy frogmen. One of them is in a biological isolation suit. While you are a hero to the world, you also might be the one person to bring upon it the greatest disaster in all of humanity's history.

▲ Apollo 11 astronauts, still in their quarantine van, are greeted by their wives upon arrival at the Ellington Air Force Base on July 27, 1969.

For one big question remains: Do you carry any alien germs for unknown illnesses that can devastate humans?

When the hatch is opened, the frogman in the biological isolation suit passes three of the same protective suits into the *Columbia*. After the three of you are secure in those suits, you join the frogman in a huge rubber raft.

You are still not cleared to join other humans. Once aboard the ship, you and the others, including the Navy frogman, scrub each other with iodine solution. This will kill any earthly viruses and bacteria. No one knows whether iodine will kill unearthly viruses or bacteria. But still, it must be done.

When you are transferred from ship to shore, you face quarantine in isolation chambers, where your future depends on a crew of white mice.

A dozen other people join you in those chambers. Their job is to test you and the moon rocks in every microscopic way possible for the existence of any kind of germ. If they find one and any of you become incurably sick, all 15 of you may well remain in those quarantine chambers for the rest of your lives.

Nothing is found that indicates alien life at a bacteria or virus level.

Still, the consequences of unleashing an unknown disease are too dire. After all, when the Black Plague hit Europe, millions upon millions of people died horrible deaths.

Days pass, and you feel no strange illness. Still, your fate depends on the colony of white mice. They were born in a laboratory and have

never been exposed to any germs. The mice are placed among the moon rocks. Then scientists monitor the mice. If they stay healthy, you will be released from quarantine to join the rest of the world.

It's not the rest of the world you want to see most. That will mean parades and speeches. There will be the 45-day "Giant Leap" tour, where you will meet presidents and kings and queens of 25 foreign countries. There will be stamps to commemorate your epic journey. Parades and speeches are an honor, of course, but how can anything ever compare to the moment of your life when you first walked on the moon?

During your quarantine, what you really miss is your family. You want to hold your spouse. You want to tell your children about those steps on the moon.

You wait. Your mind tells you that there is little chance the mice will become ill or die. After all, no germs have been detected by microscopes.

But your emotions can't be ignored. You were cramped for days in the *Columbia*. You're facing many more days in quarantine, constantly watched, like an animal in the zoo.

You want your freedom. You want your family.

Finally, nearly three weeks later, you are able to walk beyond the walls of your prison without restrictions. You are able to breathe outside air. You are able to sweep your children into your arms.

The world cheers.

But one mystery remains: those alien noises

▲ New York City welcomed the Apollo 11 crew in a ticker tape parade down Broadway and Park Avenue.

that puzzled Mission Control in Houston.

Is there something out there, between Earth and the moon? Something unknown?

No.

You wait until a news conference almost a month after Mission Control broke into your journey with an urgent question for you in the *Columbia*: "Do you hear that sound? What is it?"

At the news conference, you grin as you reveal the answer to the question that still haunts your friends in Mission Control. Those noises that led Houston to ask: "Are you sure you don't have anybody else in there with you?" They were recordings that you smuggled onto the *Columbia*. It was nothing more than a prank that still makes you giggle.

Yes. A silly prank during the most serious mission of exploration in history!

You lived your dreams as a grown-up, but you have to have the heart of a child to believe you can make it to the moon and back.

RESOURCES

I had the pleasure of learning about the Apollo 11 mission from a variety of books and magazines and website sources. You may want to begin by reading books written by the astronauts themselves, included in this list. One of the most amazing places to find out about the moon landing is the NASA website at www.nasa.gov. It has photos and videos and audio clips, and you can spend hours and hours imagining that you are part of the journey. Be sure to also check out the website for this book at Apollo11MoonMission.com.

Aldrin, Buzz, and Ken Abraham. *Magnificent Desolation: The Long Journey Home from the Moon.* London: Bloomsbury Publishing, 2009.

Aldrin, Buzz, and Wayne Warga. *Return to Earth.* New York: New York: Random House, 1973.

Allen, Bob. "A Human Computer Hidden No More." March 6, 2017 (www.nasa.gov /langley/100/launching-the -space-race-katherine-johnson).

Apollo 11: The History and Legacy of the First Moon Landing. Cambridge: Charles River Editors, 2013. Kindle edition.

Armstrong, Neil, Michael Collins, Edwin E. Aldrin Jr., and Arthur C. Clarke. *First on the Moon: A Voyage with Neil Armstrong, Michael Collins and Edwin E. Aldrin, Jr.* Boston: Little, Brown and Company, 1970. (This is the "official" memoir of the 1969 Apollo 11 moon landing mission.)

Barbree, Jay, Alan Shepard, and Deke Slayton. *Moon Shot: The Inside Story of America's Apollo Moon Landings.* New York: Open Road Integrated Media, 2011.

Beatty, Kelly. "When and How Did the Moon Form?" *Sky & Telescope.* January 13, 2017 (www.skyandtelescope.com /astronomy-news/when-and -how-did-the-moon-form/).

Braukus, Michael. "NASA Honors Apollo Engineer (Margaret Hamilton)." *NASA News.* September 3, 2003. (www .nasa.gov/home/hqnews/2003 /sep/HQ_03281_Hamilton _Honor.html).

Cavna, Michael. "Emmy Noether Google Doodle: Why Einstein Called Her a 'Creative Mathematical Genius.'" *The Washington Post.* March 23, 2015 (www.washingtonpost.com /news/comic-riffs/wp/2015/03 /23/emmy-noether-google -doodle-why-einstein-called -her-a-creative-mathematical -genius/.

Collins, Michael. *Carrying the Fire: An Astronaut's Journeys.* New York, London: Farrar, Straus and Giroux, 1974, 2009.

Collins, Michael. *Flying to the Moon: An Astronaut's Story.* New York: Farrar, Straus and Giroux, 1976.

Cortright, Edgar M. *Apollo Expeditions to the Moon: NASA's Moon Landing Program.* Washington, DC: NASA, 1975.

Dohrer, Elizabeth. "Laika the Dog & the First Animals in Space." Space.com. May 30, 2017 (www.space.com/17764-laika -first-animals-in-space.html).

EarthSky. "What Would Earth Be Like With No Moon?" December 3, 2017 (www .earthsky.org/earth/moonless -earth).

Floca, Brian. *Moonshot: The Flight of Apollo 11.* New York: Atheneum Books for Young Readers, 2013.

Gibson, Philip. *#Apollo 11: When Men Walked on the Moon.* CreateSpace Independent Publishing Platform, 2014.

Heritage Auctions. "Apollo 11 Flown Crew-Signed Commemorative Cover Directly From the Personal Collection of Mission Command Module Pilot Michael." Accessed December 10, 2017 (www.historical.ha.com/itm/explorers/space-exploration/apollo-11-flown-crew-signed-commemorative-cover-directly-from-the-personal-collection-of-mission-command-module-pilot-michael/a/6045-41069.s).

Hodges, Jim. "She Was a Computer When Computers Wore Skirts." August 26, 2008 (www.nasa.gov/centers/langley/news/researchernews/rn_kjohnson.html).

Holt, Richard. "Apollo 11 Moon Landing: Conspiracy Theories Debunked." *The Telegraph.* July 15, 2009 (www.telegraph.co.uk/news/science/space/5833633/Apollo-11-Moon-landing-conspiracy-theories-debunked.html).

Howell, Elizabeth. "The Story of NASA's Real 'Hidden Figures.'" *Scientific American.* January 24, 2017 (www.scientificamerican.com/article/the-story-of-nasas-real-ldquo-hidden-figures-rdquo/).

Kiger, Patrick J., and Marianne Spoon. "Top 10 NASA Inventions." HowStuffWorks. Accessed December 20, 2017 (https://science.howstuffworks.com/innovation/inventions/top-5-nasa-inventions.htm).

Mnagaraja. "Women's History Month Shout Out." Women@ NASA. June 21, 2012 (https://blogs.nasa.gov/womenatnasa/page/7/?x=50).

Mosher, Dave. "Millions of Dollars' Worth of Apollo Moon-Landing Gear Is Up for Auction on eBay." *Business Insider.* July 20, 2017 (www.businessinsider.com/apollo-moon-landing-ebay-sothebys-auction-2017-7).

Mosher, Dave. "President Nixon Had This 'MOON DISASTER' Speech Ready in Case Apollo 11 Astronauts Died."*Business Insider.* July 23, 2017 (www.businessinsider.com/nixon-astronaut-death-moon-disaster-speech-2017-7).

NASA. *Apollo 11 Spacecraft Commentary.* Houston, Texas: NASA Manned Spacecraft Center, 1969 (www.jsc.nasa.gov/history/mission_trans/AS11_PAO.PDF).

NASA. *Apollo 11 Technical Air-to-Ground Voice Transcription.* Houston, Texas: NASA Manned Spacecraft Center, 1969 (www.hq.nasa.gov/alsj/a11/a11transcript_tec.pdf).

NASA. "Apollo 11 Timeline." (www.history.nasa.gov/SP-4029/Apollo_11i_Timeline.htm).

NASA. "Apollo 13." July 8, 2009 (www.nasa.gov/mission_pages/apollo/missions/apollo13.html).

NASA. "Brief History of Rockets." Accessed December 15, 2017 (www.grc.nasa.gov/www/k-12/TRC/Rockets/history_of_rockets.html).

NASA Science Beta. "What Neil & Buzz Left on the Moon." May 9, 2017 (https://science.nasa.gov/science-news/science-at-nasa/2004/21jul_llr/).

Nelson, Craig. *Rocket Men: The Epic Story of the First Men on the Moon.* New York: Penguin Group, 2009.

Otto, Sasjkia. "Apollo 11 Moon Landing: Top 15 Nasa Inventions." *The Telegraph.* July 22, 2009 (www.telegraph.co.uk/news/science/space/5893387/Apollo-11-moon-landing-top-15-Nasa-inventions.html).

Rao, Joe. "10 Things You Didn't Know About the Moon." Space.com. March 18, 2011 (www.space.com/11162-10-surprising-moon-facts-full-moons.html).

Reichhardt, Tony. "Remembering Belka and Strelka." *Air & Space Smithsonian.* August 19, 2010 (www.airspacemag.com/daily-planet/remembering-belka-and-strelka-143143843/).

Schultz, Jim. "Launching the Space Race: Making Space." March 1, 2017 (www.nasa.gov/langley/100/making-space).

Sharp, Tim. "Valentina Tereshkova: First Woman in Space." Space.com. January 22, 2018 (www.space.com/21571-valentina-tereshkova.html).

Shetterly, Margot Lee. "Katherine Johnson Biography." August 3, 2017 (www.nasa.gov/content/katherine-johnson-biography).

Solar System Exploration Research Virtual Institute (SSERVI). "Simulations Show Mini-Moons Orbiting Earth." December 2, 2017. (https://sservi.nasa.gov/articles/simulations-show-mini-moons-orbiting-earth/).

Space Exploration Beta. "What Was Apollo 11's Reentry Speed at Parachute Deployment?" Stack Exchange. November 4, 2013 (www.space.stackexchange.com/questions /2661/what-was-apollo -11s-reentry-speed-at -parachute-deployment).

SpinFold. "30 Amazing Facts about the Moon." SpinFold. Accessed May 23, 2018. (www .spinfold.com/30-amazing-facts -about-the-moon/).

Stone, Randy, and Jennifer Ross-Nazzal. "The Accidents: A Nation's Tragedy, NASA's Challenge." Accessed December 3, 2017 (www.nasa.gov/centers /johnson/pdf/584719main _Wings-ch2b-pgs32-41.pdf).

Teitel, Amy Shira. "The CIA's Bold Kidnapping of a Soviet Spacecraft." *Popular Science.* October 20, 2015 (www.popsci .com/cias-bold-kidnapping -soviet-spacecraft).

Telegraph. "Apollo 11 Moon Landing: Ten Facts about Armstrong, Aldrin and Collins' Mission." *The Telegraph.* July 18, 2009 (www.telegraph.co.uk /news/science/space/5852237 /Apollo-11-Moon-landing-ten -facts-about-Armstrong-Aldrin -and-Collins-mission.html).

Thomas, Steven. *The Moon Landing Hoax: The Eagle That Never Landed.* Swordworks, 2010. Kindle edition.

Trivedi, Bijal P. "Chicago Meteor Shower a Windfall for Area Scientists." *National Geographic Today.* May 13, 2003 (https:// news.nationalgeographic.com /news/2003/05/0513_030513 _tvmeteorites.html).

Weinberger, Howard C. "Apollo Insurance Covers." Space Flown Artifacts. Accessed December 1, 2017 (www.spaceflownartifacts .com/flown_apollo_insurance _covers.html).

Television coverage of the Apollo 11 mission

The sources below show portions of the television coverage of the Apollo 11 mission. To access the links directly from your computer, go to www.Apollo11MoonMission .com/television

prelaunch

"Apollo 11 Part 2 Evening News Coverage." Filmed July 1969. YouTube Video, 07:11. Posted August 2010 (www.youtube.com /watch?v=x6m1TU-i4yY&index =2&list=PLwxFr1zAEfokQUX PUyyss0qp1Unqax5AU).

run-up to launch

"Apollo 11 Part 6 Evening News Coverage." Filmed July 1969. YouTube Video, 08:17. Posted August 2010 (https://www. youtube.com/watch?v =3mjSosOV_Mk&index=6&list =PLwxFr1zAEfokQUXPUyyss 0qp1Unqax5AU).

Photo Credits

Thanks to NASA's generosity in sharing its valuable materials with the reading public, most of the photographs in this book come from NASA's online photo archives, especially the NASA Image and Video Library at www.nasa.gov. A few of the other historic photos are public domain. Those images requiring special credit are noted below.

Title page, NASA/Jet Propulsion Laboratory (JPL)/ United States Geological Survey (USGS); page **29**, American Association of Variable Star Observers; page **33** (bottom), NASA *Watch the Skies* blog; page **47** (right), *Popular Science Monthly,* volume 76; page **48**, NASA/Apollo Training Manual "Apollo Spacecraft & Systems Familiarization," 1968; page **54**, NASA Special Publication 4205; page **56** (bottom), NASA/Aubrey Gemignani; page **58**, NASA/McREL; page **59**, NASA/JPL/USGS; page **63**, NASA Special Publication 368; page **68**, NASA/GSFC/Arizona State University; page **76**, United States Civil Air Patrol via NASA; page **77**, NASA Goddard Space Flight Center; page **78**, NASA/Bill Ingalls; page **79**, RR Auction via iCollector.com; page **88**, NASA/JPL/USGS.

Every reasonable effort has been made to trace ownership of and give accurate credit to copyrighted material. Information that will enable the publisher to correct any discrepancies is appreciated.

INDEX

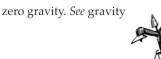

To the memory of my father, Willem Jacob Brouwer:
You never lost your childlike curiosity about the night skies,
and that will always inspire me. — SB

Text © 2019 Sigmund Brouwer
Illustrations © 2019 Barb Kelly

Kids Can Press gratefully acknowledges the financial support of the Government
of Ontario, through the Ontario Media Development Corporation; the Ontario Arts
Council; the Canada Council for the Arts; and the Government of Canada for our
publishing activity.

Published in Canada and the U.S. by Kids Can Press Ltd.
25 Dockside Drive, Toronto, ON M5A 0B5

Kids Can Press is a Corus Entertainment Inc. company

www.kidscanpress.com

The text in the book is set in Palatino and Myriad.

Edited by Kathleen Fraser
Designed by Barb Kelly

Printed and bound in Shenzhen, China, in 10/2018 by C & C Offset

CM 19 0 9 8 7 6 5 4 3 2 1

Library and Archives Canada Cataloguing in Publication

Brouwer, Sigmund, 1959–, author
    Moon Mission : the epic 400-year journey to Apollo 11 / written by
Sigmund Brouwer.

Includes index.
ISBN 978-1-5253-0036-3 (hardcover)

1. Project Apollo (U.S.) — Juvenile literature. 2. Apollo 11 (Spacecraft) —
Juvenile literature. 3. Space flight to the moon — Juvenile literature. I. Title.

TL789.8.U5A563 2019   j629.45'40973   C2018-901872-0